MW01145678

# Mindful Listening:
## How To Be Present, Intentional, and Empathetic

By Patrick King
Social Interaction and Conversation
Coach at
www.PatrickKingConsulting.com

# Table of Contents

# Introduction

Browse any self-help section in a bookstore or search YouTube for popular personal development videos, and you'll find all the familiar favorites: You can learn how to assert yourself confidently, how to flirt, and how to be charming, persuasive, and articulate, plus every other variation of "how to win friends and influence people." What you probably *won't* find is a book teaching you how to make other people feel charming, persuasive, and articulate!

This, however, is that book, and in it we'll be considering what is arguably the world's most underappreciated social skill: listening. Being a better listener may not at first appear to have any of the glamor of being a more captivating speaker, but the truth is that knowing how to listen well holds far more benefits than knowing how to express yourself.

Learning to listen—really listen—doesn't just improve your relationships, help you resolve conflicts and misunderstandings, deepen your connection to others, and enrich your work, family, and love life. It also brings a depth, color, and richness to your own life that's hard to appreciate until you experience it for yourself.

In the chapters that follow, we'll take a closer look at the many different kinds of listening, how and why to use each type, and what to do when the inevitable snags and roadblocks threaten to get in the way. We'll consider the optimal mindset to adopt so that you can become that person who is perceptive, empathetic, and easily able to connect with people of all kinds. By learning to listen, you ease your way out of bad conversational habits and start to master an approach to life and to other people that will dramatically improve your own well-being and the well-being of those around you. Step by step, you'll learn to have better conversations, to read verbal and nonverbal cues, and to hear what people are really saying when they speak (and that includes when they're lying . . .).

All that's required is an open mind, a little curiosity, and the willingness to try some of these principles out for yourself. The rewards are more than worth it.

# Chapter 1: What Are We Really Doing When We Listen?

## Cultivating "Listening Readiness"

*In this chapter: The first task of listening is to be prepared, receptive, and willing.*

Imagine that you're catching up with an old friend you haven't seen in years. The two of you meet at a busy café one morning, and perching on two uncomfortable bar chairs, you begin a disjointed conversation in between ordering, drinking, and paying for your drinks. The noise in the café means you're struggling to hear every word, and as your friend starts telling you about what's been happening in their life for the last five years, you realize your attention is drifting and you're finding the conversation boring.

Later, when you get home, you think with some disappointment that the meeting didn't go so well. You used to be great friends, but the meeting earlier that day was so awkward and lacking in connection that you're wondering if it's worth staying in touch at all.

So, what happened?

The answer is simple: a lack of preparation. Good listening and communication skills more generally are things we all take for granted—right up until they're not there, and we sorely feel their absence. Most of us understand that if you're giving a speech, you need to prepare some notes and practice; if you're attending a class, you need to come ready to take notes and pay attention; if you're sitting down to write an important email, you need to take the time to plan it all out.

Yet when it comes to communicating, we all seem to assume that this most essential skill will more or less come naturally without any planning or preparation. While we all recognize the importance of structuring our thoughts and ideas when it comes to *speaking* (or writing, teaching, etc.), we can forget that there is just as much intentionality required on the other side of things—the *listening*.

The reason we do this is because we think of speaking and writing as active, and listening as passive. We imagine that listening is simply *not doing*. And how many ways can there be of not doing anything, right?

This misconception, however, is at the heart of our misunderstanding about how to communicate better. Listening is just as important as speaking, if not more so, and it takes just as much skill, deliberation, and practice—there is nothing obvious or automatic about it!

This, then, is where we will start our mission to become more masterful, intelligent communicators. If you're like most people, chances are you've received exactly zilch in the way of formal training in listening skills. That means, sadly, that you've probably picked up plenty of misconceptions and lazy habits yourself over the years. If we continue to think that listening is easy, automatic, and not so important anyway, we will continue to fail to make any efforts to improve. We may encounter good advice that may genuinely help us communicate better, but ignore it, thinking, "That doesn't apply to me. I'm actually already a good listener."

Listening is frequently seen as an annoyance or a chore; it is undervalued or ignored. In a society that places a higher value on speaking, listeners do not receive the same level of praise, attention, instruction, or credibility as speakers. They should!

Instead, the demand to listen is often conveyed without concrete instruction—and it's often delivered as an emotional threat or power play ("You'd better listen to me!"). In our attention-depleted but individualistic culture, people are programmed to believe that listening is something you begrudgingly do for the sake of the other person, but also to earn your right to snatch back the limelight and continue to do the more interesting part— getting *them* to listen to *you*.

In this book we'll take it as a given that people are not good listeners by default. This doesn't make them unkind or selfish or stupid. You're not any of these things because you don't automatically know how to give a speech or write an essay, right? Rather, listening is a skill like any other—it requires conscious, deliberate effort. As you'll soon see, this effort is almost always rewarded with more satisfying communication, better relationships, and much less conflict and misunderstanding in life.

Returning now to our example: what went wrong? Two old friends show up to a casual location and attempt a conversation, but it fails. Hopefully you can see that the issue was simply that they were unprepared. It was taken for granted that communication would just happen all on its own—but then it didn't. A little more care and effort might have steered the encounter in a different direction entirely.

"Listening readiness" may seem an odd concept, but when we can consciously and deliberately set the scene for our conversations, we not only demonstrate our respect for the other person and the interaction we'll have with them, but we also ensure we give that interaction the best chance of success, whatever that may look like for the people involved.

Now, nobody is suggesting that you kill all spontaneity and start organizing your everyday conversations with a clipboard and a checklist. It does mean, however, no longer assuming that connection, understanding, and listening will happen on their own without effort. It means, for example, being aware that a noisy and uncomfortable café will be distracting and noisy, and purposefully choosing a place instead where you know you can talk to the person face to face in quiet privacy and comfort.

It's common to see poor listening skills blamed on narcissism or a lack of consideration for the other person. While this may indeed be the case (we'll certainly address this in later chapters), it's usually more often a question of clumsiness rather than malice. Without giving the act of listening and conversation a special place in our minds, we don't tend to stop and deliberately give it any space or attention of its own, and consequently we are rushed or distracted when we attempt to talk to people. And so, too many of us attempt difficult conversations with the TV on in the background, or juggle a conversation while looking at our phones, driving, or doing a dozen other things at the same time.

The idea of listening readiness was first introduced by Professor Nadine Marsnik and the *International Listening Association*. Such readiness is broken down into three separate categories: physical, mental, and emotional.

## Physical Preparedness, i.e., *Are you physically ready to listen?*

It may seem obvious, but even the most attentive and empathetic person is going to struggle to listen to you if they're being mauled by a lion or haven't eaten in two weeks. What might it look like to *not* be physically ready to listen?

- Being too hungry, tired, grumpy, inebriated, hot, cold, uncomfortable, or ill to pay proper attention
- Being stressed, rushed, or busy with something else
- Being too emotionally aggravated to be fully present—e.g., overly angry, sad, or scared

Physical preparedness may simply come down to making sure that the chair is comfortable, nobody is thirsty, and you're not attempting a conversation at 11 p.m. when everyone is fatigued and unable to manage a full-blown discussion about something important.

## Mental Preparedness, i.e., *Are you mentally ready to listen?*

Being able to literally comprehend the sounds coming out of the other person's mouth is only a tiny part of listening. Are you psychologically and mentally able to receive what is being shared with you?

Lacking the mental readiness to listen means:

- Not having the background knowledge to understand what you're being told— for example, missing important contextual information

- Not having a clear idea of what the conversation is for, or even that a conversation is or should be happening
- Distractions and competing thoughts and ideas (either your own or someone else's)

### Emotional Preparedness, i.e., *Are you emotionally ready to listen?*

Arguably the biggest impediment to listening is not that our ears don't work or that the chair is a little wobbly—it's that we are not emotionally willing to fully place our neutral attention and care onto the other person and the information they're trying to convey to us. In fact, most of what we'll explore in this book returns to these more insidious emotional impediments to proper listening—judgment, prejudice, and lack of empathy.

Lacking emotional preparedness looks like:

- Entering a discussion with a pre-existing agenda
- Conversations had under duress, force, or emotional manipulation—for example, one party wants to avoid it, whereas the other wants to force it
- Automatically judging someone's grammar usage, accent, or mode of expression

While it may seem like overkill to carefully consider each of these components before every conversation, the general principle is sound: Do you have a conscious, deliberate intention for how your conversations will play out, or are you just carelessly letting things unfold as they will? Picture your task merely as setting the stage. Any listening skills you develop won't matter unless you first have a properly designated time and place in which to demonstrate them.

Here are three more tips to help you better prepare that listening stage:

1. **Always approach listening as an active and intentional process that involves standing back from your own thoughts** and fully concentrating on what the other person is saying. Recognize the importance of careful listening and understand that true listening requires effort and focus.

2. **Acknowledge the significance of looking people in the eyes while they speak.** Use eye contact to lock on to the speaker's message and consciously ignore distractions and disruptions in your environment.

3. **Recognize the importance of nonverbal communication, which can account for a significant portion**

**of the overall communication experience.** Practice reading between the lines by paying attention to body language and voice inflection, as these elements often convey unspoken messages.

We will be exploring each of the above in more detail in the chapters to come, but for now, it's enough to remind yourself, as often as you can, that *listening matters*. Before you enter any conversation, think to yourself, "What do I need to do right now to make myself better prepared to listen?"

# 4 Types of Listening

*In this section: There are four main ways to listen . . . and "pseudo-listening" isn't one of them.*

Here's a story you have probably heard before, or else lived through yourself. It goes like this: During a conversation someone complains to their partner, "You're not listening to me!" The partner protests and denies this, and promptly repeats everything they've just been told, in precise detail. "See? I *was* listening."

You can probably guess that this response, however, doesn't ever convince the first partner!

Just like there are many, many different ways to speak, write, and express yourself, there are many ways to listen. Not all ways of listening are created equal, and what is appropriate in one context may not be so in another. This is why the first partner may be justified in saying, "You weren't *really* listening, though."

Knowing about the different ways to listen will help you tailor your listening style to the person in front of you, the message you're hearing, and the context you find yourself in. Each listening style is like a tool in your communication inventory that serves a distinct function. There is appreciative listening, empathic listening, comprehensive listening, and critical listening. As your skills improve, however, you will see that there are probably far more shades and nuances in the way you can listen.

### *Appreciative Listening*
### Listening for Enjoyment

Appreciative listening is when the listener focuses on deriving enjoyment from what is being communicated. This can be akin to listening to music for pleasure. Conversations involve engaging with content that brings joy, inspiration, or amusement. Examples include sermons in places of worship, motivational speeches, or stand-up comedy. Every time someone tells you a really funny or entertaining story, the ideal response is to listen in a way that actively conveys how much you're enjoying the listening.

This is because the intention of the message being shared is precisely to create this feeling of enjoyment. It's important, therefore, to not just "listen" with the intention of enjoyment, but to express and communicate this enjoyment back to the speaker.

**When to Use:** Use appreciative listening when the primary goal is to derive enjoyment or inspiration from the communication. This type is suitable for situations where the content is meant to be enjoyed, uplifted, or appreciated. For example, someone delivers an inspiring speech at a family get-together, or your grandmother shares a cute story about your childhood around the dinner table.

**TIPS:**

1. **Focus Actively.** Cease other activities, maintain eye contact, and nod affirmatively. Actively engage by refraining from distractions, signaling your attentive presence.

2. **Express Positivity.** Utilize affirmative body language—position toward the speaker, nod, and vocalize agreement. Convey positive engagement through nonverbal cues.

3. **Reflect Understanding**. Practice reflective listening. Summarize or paraphrase key points to show understanding and strengthen the connection with the speaker.

**Things to Avoid:** Whatever you do, don't focus on the factual details—these are not relevant. Don't be the "well, actually" person. For example, don't correct your grandmother and tell her the story's details don't add up or make sense, or attempt to interrupt the inspiring speech with a few comments of your own that give a more "realistic" take on events. Responding in such a way or getting overly literal will be perceived as rude and cold; you will rightly be perceived as refusing what has been offered in the spirit of a gift.

### *Empathic Listening*
### Listening for Feelings

Empathic listening revolves around showing mutual concern and understanding for the speaker's perspective—and it's frequently an *emotional* perspective. It requires being fully present in the moment, setting aside personal thoughts, and stepping into the speaker's shoes to comprehend their feelings and situation, instead of letting your own perception color things.

**When to Use:** Choose empathic listening when building relationships, offering support, or understanding someone else's emotions and experiences. This type is effective in personal conversations, conflict resolution, or situations where emotional connection is essential. Naturally, it's less appropriate in more neutral or professional contexts where emotion is not acknowledged as primary.

**TIPS:**

1. **Be Fully Present:** Provide full attention and remain impartial.

Practice receptive listening by focusing not just on the speaker's words, but on the emotional context behind them and on nonverbal cues that hint toward that person's needs, values, perceptions, and interpretation of an event.

2. **Deliberately Acknowledge Emotions.** As we will explore in a later chapter, there is value in deliberately witnessing and labeling the emotions you perceive in others. Demonstrate empathy by acknowledging and validating the person's emotions, using their own words. It can also help to thank them for their honesty and openness.

3. **Ask Reflective, Open-Ended Questions.** Demonstrate a willingness to be receptive to what's being shared with you. Pose reflective, open-ended questions that communicate loud and clear your respect for the other person's perspective, and your genuine interest in their lives.

**Things to Avoid:** Contrary to what much popular self-help may suggest, empathy is not a silver bullet for everything—not every problem can be solved by the addition of more empathy! Specifically, offer empathy and compassion only *when the other person wants it* and it's appropriate for the situation. Too many people, in their personal need to come across as kind and caring, will override another person's valid desire to not share their emotions. Alternatively, empathic listening may simply be inappropriate in the workplace or with a more superficial acquaintance.

### *Comprehensive Listening*
### Listening for Data

Comprehensive listening involves actively understanding and processing the informational content of the message. It is essential when receiving information in the form of news, lectures, or directions/instructions. The listener actively engages with the material, takes notes, and evaluates the structure and supporting evidence presented.

**When to Use:** Opt for comprehensive listening when the goal is to understand and retain information accurately. One of communication's more basic functions is simply to transfer information from one person to another. This type is essential in academic settings, professional environments, and any situation where the accurate reception and retention of information are critical. That said, it still requires all the same skills used in more empathic listening—i.e., the suspension of judgment, prejudice, and assumption.

**TIPS:**

1. **Clarify Unfamiliar Terms.** Enhance comprehension by proactively addressing unfamiliar words or concepts. If a term is unclear, ask for clarification to ensure a complete understanding of the message. For example, if someone uses a technical term that you don't understand during a presentation, you might say, "Could you please clarify the term 'XYZ'? I want to ensure I fully grasp your message."

2. **Employ Content-Oriented Evaluation.** Approach messages with scrutiny and impartial assessment. Content-oriented listeners evaluate information thoroughly, ensuring a balanced perspective. This contributes to a deeper understanding of the message.

3. **Utilize Sympathetic Listening.** In situations where understanding emotions is crucial, employ sympathetic listening. Focus on comprehending and acknowledging the

speaker's feelings rather than attempting to put yourself in their shoes. This can be a little tricky for people, but just remember that emotions themselves can also be understood as data—we can understand emotions, *and* we can feel them. Sympathy is the former, empathy the latter.

**Things to Avoid:** The biggest risk with this form of listening is its misapplication. This could mean using comprehensive listening when a more empathic mode is required, or else treating things that are not factual data as though they are—for example, failing to recognize conjecture and opinion for what it is, and responding to it as though it were neutral, objective fact.

### *Critical Listening*
Critical listening is focused on evaluating the content of the message, requiring the listener to analyze and make judgments. This type of listening is crucial in scenarios like making informed purchases or understanding complex information, where the listener assesses the validity and implications of the message.

**When to Use:** Employ critical listening when the goal is to evaluate the content, make informed decisions, or assess the validity of the information. This type is crucial in situations where critical thinking and analysis are required. You can probably see, however, that "evaluating" can be perilously close to "judging," and so this kind of listening should only be attempted when it's one hundred percent clear that your appraisal is requested and welcome.

**TIPS:**

1. **Ask Clarifying Questions.** When engaging in critical listening, ask questions to seek clarification and gather more information. For example, "I'm interested in this refrigerator, but I'm not clear about the energy efficiency. Can you explain more about its energy-saving features?"

2. **Evaluate Credibility.** Assess the credibility of the information source by considering qualifications and reliability.

3. **Consider Multiple Perspectives.** Practice critical thinking by considering different viewpoints and weighing the pros and cons.

**Things to Avoid:** This kind of "listening" is in reality the least useful and common. It's the one, however, that many of us accidentally fall into at all the wrong times. For example, someone might be sharing an upsetting story with us, and we instantly start listening to find out who is to blame. Or, perhaps, when someone is sharing their perspective on a certain idea, we immediately start thinking whether we believe it's good or bad, right or wrong, etc. A good rule of thumb is that in most human relationships, evaluation and appraisal of this kind—especially if it's a moral judgment—is almost always unnecessary.

"Critical" is a word that has a clear definition involving the neutral analysis of pros and cons, but it's no coincidence that in everyday usage, this word also means disapproving. Remember that on an emotional level, most people will automatically perceive *appraisal* as *disapproval*.

Let's return now to the couple at the beginning of the chapter, and the person who was accused of not listening even though they clearly demonstrated that they were. You may be able to see that the issue here is the *kind* of listening that was being offered. One partner requires empathic listening, and the other was perhaps offering comprehensive or critical listening.

The problem can go the other way, however. Many sensitive, caring types pride themselves on being compassionate and empathic, but are nevertheless poor listeners because they are unable to offer anything *but* this type of listening. This can be a problem when they are in situations requiring one of the other types—they will just as readily be perceived as "not listening." Real empathy, then, can be considered the ability to notice what the situation and the other person actually require of you and to respond appropriately.

### . . . And Then There's "Pseudo-Listening"

One problem is that all the above can be faked. Pseudo-listening is, simply, the mere *appearance* of listening without the deeper attention and receptivity that comes with genuine listening. Pseudo-listening can rear its head when people are aware that they *should* be listening and want to appear as though they are, but they remain uninterested in the actual listening part. This isn't always a bad thing: All of us sooner or later need to feign interest out of politeness, and "going through the motions" may indeed prove to be the easiest way through certain situations.

Pseudo-listening, however, can be more of a problem when the person doing it isn't actually aware of what they're doing—i.e., they believe they are listening. Read most how-to articles on how to be a better listener and you will almost certainly see a simple list of behaviors—external behaviors—that are designed merely to give the external appearance of thoughtful listening. We are told to make eye contact, to say "Uh huh" and "Oh really?" now and then, to not interrupt, to nod and smile, etc. The trick is, these *are* the things that people who are genuinely listening tend to do, but that doesn't mean that doing them automatically means you're listening. If you've ever been on the receiving end of this kind of thing, you'll know just how obvious it is when someone is faking it!

Pseudo-listening often comes with a tiny shred of genuine attention, as though the person is scanning selectively just in case they hear anything they actually are interested in. They may have ears pricked for things that concern them directly, or pay just enough attention to recognize when the other person asks them a question or expects a response.

If we're honest, most of us will have to admit that we do this more often than we should. Pseudo-listening is the kind of shallow attention that picks out just a few highlights and therefore often leads to misunderstandings or crossed wires. It is in fact our superficial listening that makes others seem uninteresting—a bit like skimming through a complicated novel and then complaining later that it was boring. On hearing someone speak you may think to yourself, "Yeah, yeah, I've heard this before. I know where this story is going," and then tune them out, but in doing so, you actually miss the opportunity to learn that you were wrong, and that you're about to learn something. It is your lack of engagement itself that drains the life from the conversation, and not the quality of what's being shared with you.

When it comes to pseudo-listening, there's no big secret: Just don't do it. In a later chapter, we'll be exploring the power of curiosity and how it can combat this kind of restlessness and distraction when listening to others, but for now simply be aware that pretending to listen is a waste of your time (and is seldom as convincing to the other person as you think!).

## Understanding Silence

*In this chapter: Silence gives conversations depth, meaning, and space to unfold. Don't be afraid to lean back and let people fill that space.*

Imagine that you have a close friend who comes to you with a serious problem. They're baring their soul, they're upset, and they lay out a long, complicated story at your feet. Eventually, they take a deep breath, sigh, and stop talking. They're crying a little. What do you do?

a) Change the topic and start talking about some good things happening later that week to take their mind off things.
b) Tell them a story about when and how you overcame a similar challenge yourself.
c) Give them some inspiring words of encouragement and tell them that you believe in them, whatever happens.
d) Give them a hug and tell them a joke to cheer them up.
e) Dawdle as you try to think which of the above responses to pick . . .

Often, particularly in uncomfortable or emotionally heavy conversations, we can find ourselves wracking our brains, not quite knowing what to say next. In these moments, we can forget an important option that we always have in the bag: the choice to say nothing at all.

A conversation is of course a back-and-forth, a give-and-take. It's a game of attentional tennis, where the "players" lob the topic between them, taking turns, as it were. But there is always an invisible player in this conversational game, and it's one that truly masterful conversationalists have really figured out—silence.

It's common to imagine that a "flowing" conversation is one that is going well, and to panic a little when talking lulls for a moment and things go quiet. Actually, silence plays an important, even essential role in conversations, and it's especially useful if we want to become better listeners. It may sound glib, but you cannot really hear what someone is saying if you're actively talking—or even thinking about talking. It's impossible for someone to say something unless there is an open space into which they can say it. In other words, sometimes people can't really have a conversation because they're too busy talking!

By embracing and cultivating the right kind of silence, you are opening up a space into which the other person can put their words, their thoughts, their feelings. If that space is already cluttered with your expectations, your bias, your nervous chatter, or your assumptions about what they're telling you before you've even heard it . . . then you don't have much chance of really hearing them.

Whether you want to resolve a conflict, brainstorm a new solution together, tell a story, listen empathetically, find out more about the other person, or simply enjoy an entertaining bit of banter, you are going to need to let the conversation breathe—and that requires enough silence.

The best of us can sometimes fail to listen because we have a very fixed agenda of what "good listening" looks like. A friend may come to us upset and needing to talk, and we may immediately think, "Okay, cool. Time for me to play the role of a compassionate friend. I'd better make all the right noises and give them a hug and say, '*You got this*' . . ."

Though this response comes from a place of kindness and concern, it doesn't allow the other person to spontaneously unfold the conversation in the direction it needs to go. The irony is that you may be so focused on playing out the appearance of good listening that you fail to actually listen for real. The next time you encounter a lull in the conversation and a silence appears between you, just pause for a moment and notice it there. Notice your own desire to jump in and fill the space, and just hang back for a few seconds instead. Learning how to work *with* this silence— rather than just mindlessly fill it—can help you take your conversational skills to the next level.

- Silence gives them **time to think**, to feel. It gives you time to do the same, to digest and process what is happening, and to reflect rather than barge ahead.
- Silence builds **trust**. It tells people, in a deep and sometimes counterintuitive way, "I see you. Just as you are, just as things are, right now. I'm here with you."
- Silence communicates a presence and a tacit **acceptance**, because we are not trying to fix or change anything. We are not treating the present moment like something to quickly hurry on from or label or judge.
- Silence lets us **slow down** and take a step back. This can allow us to see creative solutions to problems we may not have noticed before.
- Silence **empowers** people. It sends the message loud and clear that you believe the other person can and will help themselves, without needing you there to talk and fix and solve for them.

- Silence makes us **curious** and receptive. Instead of rushing to some conclusion just for the sake of it, we pause a moment in ambiguity and open-endedness and allow ourselves instead to ask questions.
- Silence helps us normalize and **cope** with strong emotions. With your silence you demonstrate that you can hold and contain emotions. When you chatter and nervously fill the silence, it's often because on some level, you don't accept the emotional reality and cannot "sit with" it. On the other hand, being silent in the face of someone's strong emotion can help people feel more able to accept it in themselves.
- Silence **takes the pressure off** us. We remember that we are not responsible for everything and everyone, and we don't have to come up with perfect solutions in a split second. We can take our time. We can choose *not* to respond.

By now, most of us know that it's bad to interrupt. If we're honest, though, how often do we interrupt people *mentally*? In other words, how often do we allow our own internal chatter to start up and interfere with our ability to hear what the other person is saying? We may be externally silent, but internally we are actually prioritizing *listening to ourselves* instead of them. Even before they've finished, we are preparing and rehearsing a response to them, or chattering away to ourselves in response. Whether we interrupt in an obvious or not-so-obvious way, though, the effect is the same: We do not give the other person enough space. We cannot hear them.

So, the next time you're having a conversation with someone, pay special attention to the little silences—start to see them as possible invitations to go a bit deeper. Your response to temporary lulls in conversation can actually steer things in different directions, creating more rapport, understanding, and empathy. When you start noticing all these little spaces, you might realize just how many different things you can do with them!

### Ways You Can Respond to Silence

Be still and let the silence be. Hold it for five to ten seconds. Don't merely give the impression that you're thinking about what they just said. Genuinely think about it!

### Remember Body Language

While pseudo-listening is no good, spare a thought for what you may still be communicating nonverbally. You can be completely silent but nevertheless express an incredible level of engagement and focus simply by maintaining eye contact, an appropriate facial expression, and open body language angled toward the speaker.

**Forget Yourself**

You could use a quiet moment to consider what you think about what's being shared. But what happens when you instead think about what *they're* feeling? Try to go deeper into their experience. Why did they pause at this exact moment? What do you imagine is running through their mind right now? How do they feel?

The interesting thing about switching your focus from yourself to them is how comfortable and easy it makes silences. You may realize that people instantly become a whole lot more interesting to you once you stop trying to decide what you think of them and instead consider what they think of you!

**Consider Your Next Move**

A conversation is like walking a unique path through a maze. At any point you can stop, consider the crossroads in front of you, and decide which direction to take things. In the silence, pause a beat and ask yourself what the conversation needs, what you need, what they need.

If they seem distracted, bored, or restless, you might like to break the silence or end the conversation until a better time.

If they suddenly make eye contact and seem to be searching your face, they may want you to say something next.

If they're upset or crying, try to imagine what they're feeling and check to see if some physical contact, kind words or a hug might be warranted.

If they seem awkward, uncomfortable, or struggling to speak, you might need to address it directly: "Is there anything you want to talk about?" or "What's on your mind?"

If they seem angry or unhappy about the silence, you don't have to apologize or rush to say something. "Well, I was just listening to you" or "I'm thinking about what you said" is honest and often gives people permission to speak frankly and be heard—something they may not be used to!

If someone has just been very vulnerable with you or shared something very important or difficult, give it a few seconds before you respond—it will convey a sense of respect for what you've heard.

**Use Silence Wisely**

Of course, not all silence is golden. If you're genuinely unable to say anything interesting, if you're tired, in a bad mood, or just unable to fully engage, then be upfront about it and see if you can postpone the conversation to a better time. Likewise, just because you are comfortable with silence and can manage a more in-depth and serious conversation, it doesn't mean that the other person is ready to do the same. Respect a person's choice to continue speaking superficially, change the topic, or end a conversation they feel uncomfortable in.

Sometimes people just want to talk and be heard. Sometimes people just don't want to talk. Silence is only useful when everyone is comfortable with it, and when it is generative and supports connection and empathy. If the silences are getting longer and longer, and one or both of you is beginning to feel the strain, it could simply be a sign to gracefully bow out and pick things up at another time. That's completely normal!

**Summary**
- The first task of listening is to be prepared, receptive, and willing. Good listening requires that we are prepared in the same way as if we were planning to give a speech or write an email. Listening readiness comes in three categories: physical,

mental, and emotional. Take care to properly set the stage in each category.

- Listening is not passive and is as important as speaking, requiring as much skill, deliberation, and practice. Most of us receive no training on how to listen, or wrongly assume we don't need to learn. Listening is a skill that can be learned, and the reward is more satisfying communication, better relationships, and less conflict.
- There are four main ways to listen: *appreciative* (focusing on deriving enjoyment from what is being communicated), *empathetic* (showing concern and understanding for the speaker's emotional perspective), *comprehensive* (understanding and processing the informational content of the message), and *critical* (evaluating the content of the message, appraising, and making judgments). All approaches have value; the skill comes with being able to tailor your approach to the unique situation you're in and the other person's needs.
- Pseudo-listening is the mere *appearance* of listening without the deeper attention and receptivity that comes with genuine listening—avoid it!

- Always remember that you have the option to stay silent (that includes mentally). Silence creates space, allows possibilities to unfold, and lets a conversation "breathe."

## Chapter 2: Roadblocks to Masterful Listening

*In this chapter: No matter how top-notch your listening skills are, communication can fail if it's hijacked by too much noise.*

So, what are we doing when we listen? We're setting the scene, we're preparing ourselves, and we're opening a little space into which a conversation—a genuine conversation—can happen.

While that sounds so easy on paper, why does it so often go wrong?

In this chapter we'll look at the most common obstacles to quality listening so that you can ensure you're not being derailed by them. We can fail to truly listen when we are too occupied with our own thoughts and feelings, or when we are not open and receptive enough to other peoples'. But there's another common pitfall to listening that is not acknowledged as often, and it's a simple one . . .

**NOISE!**

Richard West and Lynn Turner are so interested in the phenomenon of noise in conversations that they've identified four different types in their 2010 book on interpersonal communication.

**Physical Noise**

Physical noise includes all the external sounds that create interference in the communication process. Picture a scenario where two colleagues are trying to discuss an important project in a bustling restaurant during peak time. The background noise of chatter, clinking cups, and the clatter of cooking in the kitchen may all create significant physical noise, making it challenging for the colleagues to hear each other clearly. Add to this the beeping of a phone or the distant hum of construction work outside and you start to appreciate just how much this obvious type of noise can disrupt effective communication.

Importantly, the noise doesn't have to be deafening or literally drown out the other person's voice to be disruptive. Any noise makes a small demand on our attention, and we only have so much bandwidth to process all these different stimuli. The more that goes to random sounds in the environment, the less we have available for the person talking in front of us.

## Physiological Noise

Physiological noise pertains to biological factors that hinder the transmission or reception of messages. Consider an individual with a severe cold attempting to explain a complex idea. The congestion and discomfort associated with the illness become physiological noise, impeding the clarity of their speech and potentially causing the listener to miss key points. Similarly, someone with articulation problems, such as a stutter, faces challenges in expressing themselves clearly, introducing physiological noise that affects the communication exchange.

## Semantic Noise

Semantic noise arises from difficulties in understanding the meaning of words or symbols in communication. You may have trouble "hearing" the meaning of a sentence due to the jumble of unnecessary verbal clutter in the way! In a professional setting, the use of industry-specific jargon without explanation can create semantic noise, as can excessive politeness, verbosity, or avoidant/circuitous language. For instance, a software developer discussing intricate coding techniques with a marketing professional may encounter semantic noise if the technical terms used are unfamiliar to the nontechnical audience.

Furthermore, improper grammar or ambiguous language can contribute to semantic noise, hindering the accurate interpretation of the intended message. For example, the sentence "I'm sure nobody here would ever disagree with the fact that you can't not say yes to the proposal you've just made" is one that actually interferes with a person's ability to comprehend its meaning!

**Psychological Noise**

Psychological noise involves mental and emotional factors that disrupt effective communication. Imagine a heated discussion about a controversial topic where strong emotions such as anger or fear are present. These emotions act as psychological noise, clouding individuals' judgment and making it difficult for them to objectively comprehend the viewpoints of others. People may be primed to interpret neutral or confusing stimuli in particular ways, to fail to recognize information that doesn't align with their pre-existing expectations, or to simply have a hard time reconciling the message with their perception of the person delivering the message.

Personal biases, whether conscious or unconscious, can introduce psychological noise by influencing how information is perceived, leading to misunderstandings and barriers in communication—especially those that feed off and amplify one another.

Naturally, you can imagine a situation where all four of these kinds of noise are operating at once. A common issue can occur when people realize that the other person is not in fact listening to them—but they jump to conclusions about why. They may wrongly assume, for example, that the person is uninterested or being deliberately difficult. People with hearing difficulties can sometimes find themselves creating subtle feelings of irritation and hostility for precisely this reason—it's difficult for people to be repeatedly asked "What!?" without it beginning to feel like they themselves are not "heard" on a psychological level, that they are unintelligible, difficult to understand, or obscure. Our message may be unheard for many reasons—but it seems human to immediately take things personally or assume malice.

### *Overcoming Noise*
### Identify the Type of Noise

Just as there are many types of silence, there are many types of noise. Which one are you dealing with? We will be discussing misunderstandings of all types throughout this book, but it's often the case that a conflict or misunderstanding stems from a simple difficulty right at the beginning of communication—i.e., you literally cannot hear one another over the noise.

If communication is difficult, empathy is lacking, or you've got a conflict on your hands, start by figuring out what is causing the disruption. Whatever you do, don't automatically assume malice or disinterest on their part. Once you know where the noise is coming from and what kind of noise it is, you can begin to deal with it productively.

**Understand the Noise and How It's Impacting You**

Obviously, your goal is to remove the noise so you can get to the important work of really connecting to the other person and what they're sharing. This will depend on the noise type.

If there's a physical noise in the environment, remove it or remove yourselves from the environment. If necessary, postpone your discussion for another time. For physiological noise, consider making accommodations for individuals with illnesses or speech impairments, or, again, wait till conditions are better. In the case of psychological noise, the most important thing is *to be aware* of emotional factors and biases. This kind of noise does its damage primarily because people are unaware it's there in the first place. Empathy and compassion are important, but even before that, you need to actually know what to be empathetic and compassionate *about*. See if you can identify and remove the more obvious things getting in the way of genuinely encountering the other person, and them encountering you.

If there is too much of a language or understanding barrier, you may need to do a lot of groundwork to agree on some shared definitions, goals, and understandings first. If there is fear, suspicion, pre-existing upset, or blame, your first task is to clear this up. This can prove extremely difficult because the way you clear it up may entail more communication—which is challenging because everyone is emotional and defensive! A time-out can work wonders, as can a neutral third party to act as a moderator.

Having said all this, the barrier may lie more squarely with you. It takes an enormous amount of maturity to recognize and take ownership of the fact that you are undermining communication, but if you can do so, you may be amazed at how much trust and rapport it inspires in the other person. It often only takes one party to "lay down their weapons" and express a sincere desire to connect, to inspire the other party to do the same. Whether you have the tiniest misunderstanding or a serious feud or dispute, the principles are the same. Again, it's as though you are clearing a space for healthy connection to happen. Trying to communicate when there's any kind of noise is like trying to drive on a road that's covered with fallen trees and rubble—i.e., liable to cause accidents!

## Plan Ahead and Minimize Obstacles

As part of your preparation and "listening readiness," be aware of potential sources of noise and plan ahead to reduce their impact. Note, however, that the best you can usually do is minimize these obstacles and seldom remove them entirely. Being proactive in this way will help you make the most of any interaction, but even if you're not one hundred percent effective, your ability to demonstrate a collaborative and problem-solving approach is often enough on its own to inspire trust and rapport in the other person. In other words, the genuine *intention and willingness* to listen is often valuable even when it doesn't entirely work!

Before we move on, it's worth considering an obstacle that's almost certainly a part of your world: technology. Being aware of how your gadgets help or hinder your connection to others is a big aspect of being a good communicator. Think carefully about exactly how certain habits around media, social media, phones, etc. are influencing your ability to pay attention, and then take the necessary steps to remove that "noise." For example, switch off or put away phones during conversations, make sure there are no distracting notification noises, or even suggest a face-to-face chat even though an email or message would be more convenient—when you think about it, considerable noises of all kinds can creep in when you are forced to communicate a delicate topic through text alone.

# The Closeness-Communication Bias

*In this chapter: You may actually be worse at listening to people you know well—be aware of this and adjust yourself accordingly.*

The closeness-communication bias refers to a phenomenon where the closer we feel to someone, the less likely we are to listen carefully to what they are saying, because our familiarity with them makes us feel like we already know what they're going to say. Part of this bias is the tendency to assume that our communication with people close to us is actually better than it really is.

The concept was explored in a study published in the *Journal of Experimental Psychology* in 2011. Savitsky and colleagues explained how egocentrism is actually higher amongst friends and family than it is amongst strangers:

> *"People commonly believe that they communicate better with close friends than with strangers. We propose, however, that closeness can lead people to overestimate how well they communicate, a phenomenon we term the closeness-communication bias. In one experiment, participants who followed direction of a friend were more*

*likely to make egocentric errors—look at and reach for an object only they could see—than were those who followed direction of a stranger. In two additional experiments, participants who attempted to convey particular meanings with ambiguous phrases overestimated their success more when communicating with a friend or spouse than with strangers. We argue that people engage in active monitoring of strangers' divergent perspectives because they know they must, but that they 'let down their guard' and rely more on their own perspective when they communicate with a friend."*

This is a fascinating finding because it suggests that we are worse at communication not because we lack the care, concern, or kindness needed to listen properly to others. Instead, it is precisely our liking and familiarity with people that makes us more careless in how we communicate with them. Conversational narcissism, then, can be more of a cognitive bias than malice, lack of care, or deliberate selfishness. We don't listen because we think we don't *need* to—we know this person and therefore we already know what they're saying.

This is akin to the experience of traveling a familiar route repeatedly; eventually, we stop noticing signposts and scenery because we believe we know the route well. The route could drastically change, and we could completely fail to notice. Have you ever met an old, divorced couple where one of them says, "I complained for years and nothing changed, so I left," while the other one says, "It came out of the blue. They left without warning, and I never saw it coming"? Perhaps the closeness-communication bias can help us understand why!

It's completely understandable that human beings start to rely on assumptions and predictions for how their loved ones will behave, rather than observing their behavior from scratch in every single interaction. Mental heuristics or shortcuts like this save brainpower and are often fairly accurate. The real problem with this bias is that people are constantly changing. And that means that the people we know inside out today may be less familiar to us tomorrow.

To communicate well, you need to make a concerted effort to remind yourself that the other person is not you; they may not know what you know or think what you think. They may not understand what you mean, or they may interpret it in completely unexpected ways. When you're close to someone, however, you may relax and make less of this effort:

- You do less perspective-taking.
- You overestimate how much you share a common frame of reference.
- You may overestimate how well you're currently understanding one another.

Friends, partners, and spouses usually *are* similar to one another, but we may lull ourselves into a false sense of just how much. We may end up using our own beliefs, thoughts, and feelings as a stand-in for those of our friends and loved ones. We like them, and so we just assume they agree with us. Then, we are surprised when we stumble on misunderstandings, even conflicts. We have not failed in our communication because we don't know them well enough. The irony is that we failed because we know them too well and have taken too much for granted.

The sum of daily interactions and activities continuously shapes individuals, so they are not the same as they were in the past. When we succumb to the closeness-communication bias, we risk overlooking the evolving nature of those close to us. This can lead to misunderstandings, as we may fail to recognize changes in perspectives, emotions, or actions. It can go the other way, too, of course: We may be subtly changing day to day in many ways, but we fail to communicate any of this directly with them, assuming that they will just naturally be in sync with us and up to date with how we currently think and feel.

And so, in romantic relationships, partners might start feeling like they don't really know each other anymore. In parent-child relationships, parents may be suddenly surprised to discover that their children are engaging in activities or behaviors they hadn't anticipated. This sudden realization of difference can be isolating, upsetting, or bewildering—but it's not strictly a problem. The problem is that our expectations fail to prepare us for it, and we start to interpret the mismatch as a threat, a kind of deception, or a loss.

What's the solution, then?

Human relationships are fascinating. We "know" someone, but that someone is a living, breathing, dynamic human being who is changing day to day, sometimes moment to moment. What this means is that to continue to know someone, we need to continue to communicate with them! We need to switch our mindset from assuming that our connection with someone is banked and automatic, and instead realize that a relationship of any kind is a continuously unfolding phenomenon. To maintain healthy relationships, it's crucial to remain attentive and open-minded, even as closeness and familiarity develop. We have to learn, in a way, to communicate anew with them in every conversation. To let go of assumptions and expectations and simply receive the person in front of us, as they are, right now.

### *Communicating with a "Beginner's Mind"*

In Zen Buddhism, the concept of beginner's mind is about cultivating a lack of preconceptions in one's approach to life. By dropping our assumptions, biases, and prejudgments (i.e., everything we think we already know), we give ourselves the chance to encounter reality *as it really is*, fresh and new and wild in each new moment.

We can bring this open-minded, curious, even playful attitude to our communication. In the context of the closeness-communication bias, we can counter some of the effects of familiarity by adopting a beginner's mind when we sit down to talk to someone. Start by asking yourself the following questions:

## What Assumptions Are You Making?

Yes, you *are* making assumptions! It's just a question of which ones you're making and how well they're serving you. It's not wrong to make assumptions, but they can be dangerous if you're making them unconsciously and mistaking them for neutral, objective observations.

Common assumptions include:

- Thinking that the other person automatically understands what you mean—for example, that they know the words and terms you're using or that they use them in exactly the same way as you do.
- Thinking that the other person will naturally agree with you—or that they already do agree, and their silence is just because this agreement is obvious to everyone.
- Thinking that the other person possesses the same knowledge about this topic as you do, or that they have all the necessary context to come to the same conclusion as you.
- Thinking that the other person shares your values, your interests, your goals, or your emotional reactions to the topic at hand.

Imagine two friends walking down a busy city street, who then pass a strange-looking preacher thumping a Bible and yelling in a language neither of them can even identify. The first friend says, "Jeez, can you believe this guy? How rude." The second friend nods and says, "I agree." The two friends walk on, happily, seemingly in agreement. But the first friend actually meant, "It's wrong to preach your religion out in public like that, and to be so inconsiderate of people walking by," whereas the second friend actually meant, "It's so rude to deliver a sermon in a language nobody understands, because then the people walking by can't enjoy it."

## Are You Being Open-Minded?

Being open-minded is like being a good driver. Everyone thinks they are a better-than-average driver, even though this is statistically impossible! Being closed-minded in the context of listening is entering a conversation expecting a particular response from the other person. You may expect this response based on an illusion of pre-existing understanding. You may, for example, share a news story that riled you up, wholly expecting that the other person will be exactly as riled as you were to hear it. Usually, we're not aware of just how narrow-minded we've been until someone goes and behaves like a free and autonomous human being! "Oh, yes, I read that news story . . . I loved it and thought it made some good points."

## Are You Being Clear Enough?

So much of human communication rests on shortcuts, symbols, hints, and insinuations. Intelligent adults know that many conversations happen "between the lines" and that it's normal to fill in the blanks. The trouble is, people tend to fill in the blanks with whatever they have at hand—and that's usually their own assumptions, preconceived ideas, and so on. We cannot expect people to come to their own conclusions and have those conclusions exactly mirror ours. It may feel a little unnatural at times, but try to be as clear and concise as possible, especially if it's a high-stakes conversation.

## Are You Wanting People to Be Mind Readers?

Magically knowing what someone thinks or feels without them saying so is overrated. People tend to valorize the ability of some people to just "get" one another, but this kind of extrasensory perception is usually more illusion than fact—it often reflects people's *belief and perception* that they have had their minds read, rather than real mind reading. Some people may even place a high value on others being able to successfully guess what they want and need. Spoiler alert: these people often find themselves sorely misunderstood and disappointed!

We communicate precisely so that we don't have to waste time guessing. Remind yourself that there is nothing special about magically mind reading other people's thoughts, and it seldom happens anyway. Not being able to read a person's thoughts doesn't mean you don't care about them or don't know them well. It's not a reflection of your grasp of them, but on their human complexity. Ask yourself honestly if you are hoping or expecting (even daring, perhaps?) other people to try to discern what you mean. Similarly, don't automatically assume you know what other people are thinking and feeling without them saying it out loud.

## Response Preparation

*In this chapter: Mentally preparing a response to what someone is saying while they're saying it is robbing them of the attention they're entitled to in a conversation—it also robs you of the attention needed to be articulate.*

In the previous chapter, we saw that one of the biggest obstacles to proper listening is the belief that we already know what is going to be shared with us. In this chapter, we'll consider one more major roadblock: trying to respond quickly to a message before we've even really heard it.

The effect goes as follows: Preparing your response to what someone is telling you while they're telling you leads to more cognitive strain. The increase in cognitive strain means you have less attention and brainpower to spend on articulating your thoughts and on listening further to what you're being told.

Response preparation, then, is like shooting yourself in the foot. If you zone out a little to mentally plan your response while the other person is still talking, you interfere both with your ability to hear the rest of that message, as well as your ability to articulate your response when it's your turn to speak. So, while we call it "response preparation," you are actually expending effort to be *worse* at responding, not to mention losing focus on the message being shared with you.

This premature focus on response detracts attention from the speaker's communication, diverting cognitive resources toward personal thoughts rather than the comprehension of the ongoing discourse. Consequently, you risk missing crucial details and nuances in the speaker's message, diminishing the overall quality of their understanding (plus, it's not as fun for you!).

In a paper by Hargie et al. (2011), the authors explain how our capacity to process spoken information is actually much greater than the rate at which information is normally delivered. So, while people tend to speak at a rate of approximately 150 words a minute, our brains are capable of processing anywhere from 400 to 800 words a minute!

What this means is that our brain has extra processing power for periphery tasks that have nothing to do with the other person's message. Now, if you only consider a conversation to be an exchange of words per minute, then you might think, "Great! I don't have to give my undivided attention, and I can think of other interesting things while this person blabs on . . ."

A conversation, however, is much, much more than the rate of data delivery. A conversation includes massive amounts of nonverbal information, emotional content, subtext, and potential interpretations. Artificial intelligence chatbots have to process thousands of possible branching pathways that even the most basic human conversation can take, and predict and update their position constantly.

In other words, in a natural human conversation, there really isn't any processing power to spare—if your mind is wandering, then it is because you are superficially processing the conversation, and not that the conversation itself is superficial. The moment you get lost in your own head, planning a response or rebuttal, is the moment you disconnect from the conversation and break that precious thread of connection.

There are a few signs that this may be a problem for you (and to be honest, it's a problem for many of us):

1. You often find yourself bored in conversations, no matter who you're talking to. Of course, some people truly are boring, but if you're finding *everyone* boring, the common denominator is you. Your boredom may

be a symptom and not a cause of a wandering and unfocused mind.

2. You often accidentally interrupt people to complete their thoughts for them, only to discover that you've misunderstood.

3. You talk too quickly and try to convey too much information at once. This can be a sign of having constructed a complete and pre-made opinion to deliver all at once, rather than a single contribution to a give-and-take conversation.

4. For the same reason, you sometimes hog the conversation and slip into "preaching" or lecture mode.

5. Your response feels jumbled, confused, and inarticulate. Somehow, you always think of the right way to say something long after the conversation is over.

6. Your responses mimic people you've watched/heard on social media, TV, podcasts, etc. rather than match and reflect the tone of the unique conversation you're presently in. This can be a sign that you are presenting a favorite canned response to the situation you assume you're in, rather than responding genuinely and spontaneously to what is in front of you.

7. You sometimes respond to something someone said a while back, rather than their most recent contribution—a dead giveaway that in the meantime you've been processing your response to an old conversational thread and ignoring the current one.

8. Finally, you are often self-conscious and worried about how you will come across to others when you respond, rather than actually listening to them. As you hyperfocus on how you might appear, you disconnect from the flow of the interaction.

### *How to Switch Gracefully into Response Mode*

If you're listening properly, there will be a slight but definite "gear switch" when you stop listening and start to respond. Just like changing gears in a car, this is a question of timing and grace.

### Plan Ahead

Take the time to think about what you want to say before a meeting or conversation even begins. Use this time to plan your thoughts and organize key points. The idea is not to do all this processing while listening, so when it's time to listen, you are ready to listen without distraction. That said, you are only outlining key points here, not a word-for-word rehearsal.

**Slow Down**

There's absolutely no rule that you have to respond the very second the other person stops speaking. In fact, giving yourself a short pause after they speak demonstrates that you're thoughtfully processing their message and are not in some mad hurry to add your own. More importantly, even a few seconds' pause gives you time to think and deliver a clearer, more organized response. Breathe deeply and take your time. People are more patient than you think, and what feels like a long pause to you may register as rather brief for others.

If you're unsure about a question or topic, don't hesitate to simply ask for clarification. It's perfectly okay to say, "Let me think about this," or even, "I don't know. I'm not sure." Expressing the need for a moment to think before responding may actually increase trust and liking because it shows you're willing to hold your tongue unless you actually have something to say.

**Be Mindful of the Media You Consume**

The way you speak and express yourself is heavily influenced by the way you are spoken to. It's worth remembering, then, that most of us today receive most of our information not from other human beings, but from various forms of media. Unconsciously and automatically, we may end up emulating the vocabulary, style, substance, and tone of the content we most often consume. If the bulk of your "communication" is one-dimensional and done with disembodied screens and apps, then it's inevitable that your communication style will reflect this: Your attention will be weak and superficial, and your field of perception will be narrowed.

If the dominant mode you find yourself in is one where you are a mere passive consumer of entertainment, or material that you have already taught an algorithm is allowed into your filter bubble, then you will be ill-equipped to engage with a real-life human being who is not behaving in any way you're familiar with. You may find yourself stumped if they're expressing ideas you may not like or immediately understand and in ways you personally don't find convenient. In other words, prioritizing media consumption over human interaction will make you a better media consumer and a worse communicator!

If you can, be mindful of not just the content you're consuming, but its form and function and the effects it has on your ability to think and to express yourself. More and more, people are realizing that the quality of their thought and perception is heavily impacted by their tech habits and the media they're exposed to. You can counter this by either cutting back drastically or deliberately exposing yourself to a wider variety of materials.

In addition, **read**. Engage in a variation of materials to expand not only your vocabulary and sentence structures, but your patience, intellectual maturity, and capacity to think critically. Read fiction and nonfiction, read from all historical periods, and read controversial or unknown material. Read things you find strange or difficult or unpleasant, as well as things that inspire and impress you.

Engage with things you don't necessarily agree with, or ideas that haven't been put in your orbit by businesses that stand to profit from your attention to them. Practice writing down thoughts and ideas to reinforce clarity and organization. Slow down. Give yourself ample time to just sit with your thoughts, stimulation-free, and practice the art of ordering and expressing your thoughts.

**Summary**

- Noise can derail even the best-laid conversational plans. There are four types of noise: *physical* (environmental distractions), *physiological* (biological discomfort and impediments), *semantic* (difficulties understanding the meaning of words or symbols in communication), and *psychological* (emotional overwhelm). Carefully identify potential noise sources and proactively prepare to remove them before listening.
- The closeness-communication bias means that the closer we feel to someone, the less likely we are to listen carefully to them, because our familiarity makes us feel like we already know what they're going to say. Be aware of this and commit to truly listening with an open mind. People change, and you cannot take agreement and similarity as a given.
- Adopt a beginner's mind and drop your assumptions, biases, and expectations. Be clear and open-minded and don't expect others to be mind readers.
- Mentally preparing your response to what someone is telling you while they're telling you increases cognitive strain and decreases the overall attention and brainpower you have to spend on articulating your thoughts and to listening to what you're being told.

- Instead, slow down, listen first, *then* gracefully go into response mode. Be mindful of the media you consume (books, social media, TV, etc.) and how this may be influencing (or undermining) your communication style.

# Chapter 3: Ask Your Ego to Take a Back Seat

## Interrupting Is a Power Play

*In this chapter: Without a doubt, the biggest obstacle to high-quality listening is a big, fat ego! One of the easiest ways to drop your ego is to unlearn the interrupting habit.*

People can be poor listeners for a whole host of reasons:

- They're unprepared for listening and have no plan to do so.
- They're listening, but in the wrong way for the situation they're in.
- They're afraid of or uncomfortable with silence.
- They're trying to listen, but they're getting drowned out by physical, physiological, semantic, or psychological noise.
- They don't think they need to listen because they already know what's being said.

- They're too busy thinking of how they'll respond to actually listen to what they're responding to.

Granted, all the above reasons are perfectly human, and most of us have been guilty of one or all of them at one point or another. It's understandable. In this chapter, however, we're exploring some of the less forgivable offenses when it comes to listening, and all of them have to do with one thing: our ego.

When we allow our ego to dominate our communication efforts, we are essentially viewing conversation as a competition or even a battle. We see ourselves or our ideas as entering an arena where they must fight and defeat other ideas so that we can ultimately feel that we've "won" the conversation. What do we win? The feeling that we're superior. Whether this feeling comes from a place of pure narcissism or a place of fear and insecurity (yes, some of the most self-centered people are deeply vulnerable and anxious) doesn't matter—the effect on communication is the same.

The way we approach communication in general stems from our deeper philosophical attitude to other people in general. Our communication style reflects the relationship we have with ourselves, with other people, with the world in general. It speaks directly to our values, our goals, and our blind spots.

Good communicators are fundamentally at peace with themselves and are able to view other people with relaxed interest and genuine respect. They see conversations as pleasant opportunities to learn, to connect, to bond. They do not tend to see difference or the unknown as a threat. Instead, they approach it with humility and curiosity. They are turned outward toward the world.

Poor communicators are fundamentally uncomfortable with themselves and are therefore uncomfortable with others, viewing them with suspicion, judgment, or fear. They can't help but see conversations as zero-sum—i.e., the other person is not someone to collaborate with, but to compete with or even defend against. The unknown is a threat that needs to be conquered. They are turned not outward toward the world, but inward, toward themselves.

That leads us to one of the biggest threats to healthy communication—interrupting. If you are a poor communicator, you may unconsciously believe that the goal of a conversation is to be the one who speaks the most and brings everyone around to your opinion. That means that any time someone else is speaking, they're winning and you're not! In other words, with your ego steering the conversation, interrupting *makes logical sense*.

With your ego kept in check, however, you understand that another person expressing themselves—even to say something you don't like or agree with—is actually not the end of the world. In fact, you can thoroughly enjoy listening to others, not speaking, and even occasionally changing your position to adopt theirs. Crazy but true.

The act of interrupting, whether intentional or not, is basically a power play in communication. While it can be a useful tactic in certain situations to assert yourself, frequent interruptions may convey a disregard for others' thoughts and a belief that one's own ideas take precedence. Any conversation is made of layers of communication: There is the outward verbal content, but also hidden emotional, cultural, and social dynamics at play, too. Interrupting is the nonverbal way to say, "What I'm saying is more important than what you're saying. I'm more important than you."

Gender dynamics play a role, too, with studies indicating that men tend to interrupt more than women—and men tend to interrupt women more than they interrupt other men, and more than women interrupt other women (Hancock & Rubin, 2014).

Not all interruptions are ego-driven. Sometimes, we blurt out something because we're excited, we're impatient for cognitive closure (for example, we're in a hurry to finish someone's sentence for them), or we're socially anxious. Some theorists suggest that there's a strong cultural element to interrupting, too, with certain cultures interjecting frequently to show support for a speaker's story, while in another culture this would be considered the height of rudeness. Ironically, interrupting may be an attempt to connect with others by sharing similar experiences, but it often leads to disengagement and frustration.

Chronic interruption can become a toxic communication habit, eroding relationships over time. If you interrupt others enough, there are usually only two responses available to them: resorting to interrupting you back, which turns the conversation into a tug-of-war, or else giving up speaking at all, in which case the connection fizzles out and you find yourself in a monologue.

Are you an interrupter? Acknowledging the behavior is a first step, but adopting strategies to enhance dialogue skills and afford others the space to express themselves is crucial. How you overcome this habit depends a lot on the underlying reasons.

If you're nervous or anxious, and you interrupt simply because your brain is going a thousand miles an hour and you're racing ahead to add your response, then the solution is clear: Relax! Challenge yourself to go into your very next conversation with the sole intention of listening, and that's all. Notice how letting the other person shine actually lowers your anxiety, whereas trying to think of something interesting or intelligent to say only increases it.

If you tend to interrupt because you get excited and over-engaged, try to retain that excitement but limit your response to shorter supporting statements like "Oh wow" or "Yeah?" or "Tell me more." Often, this kind of interruption is not really intended as an interruption at all; it just feels like one to the person trying to speak. Be a little more mindful and deliberately see yourself as supporting and encouraging the speaker, but with your facial expressions and body language instead.

If you interrupt because you genuinely feel that what you have to say is more interesting, important, or relevant, then the issue will take a little more effort to overcome. You may need to be honest about the mindset you're bringing to social situations more generally. You cannot convey a sense of respect for someone if you don't actually feel that respect. This means that breaking the interrupting habit is about changing your attitude; your behavior will follow suit.

One of the best ways to improve is simply to practice. When our ego is in charge, it convinces us that we won't be heard unless we talk loudly or a lot, and that we won't be valued or listened to unless we forcefully make our argument. The only way to teach yourself that this isn't really true is to create experiences that prove it—i.e., experiences where listening to someone else talk is genuinely enjoyable, valuable, and useful to you. Here are some ideas for challenging the ego when it rears its head in conversations:

**Treat them like the most important person in the room.** Before you begin any conversation, mentally remind yourself to imagine that the person you're speaking to is actually the most important person in the room . . . or the world, if you like! Imagine that they have something fascinating and ultra-valuable to teach you, but you just haven't figured out what it is yet. Imagine you're going to be quizzed later about what they tell you, or

79

that they're a celebrity or VIP. When you hang on to every word they say, you're less likely to interrupt.

**Focus on the speaker's words.** Make a conscious effort to deeply understand their message and emotions, which helps you stay engaged without feeling the need to interrupt. Even if you think you've got the gist of their message, assume that you don't *totally* understand it, and keep asking questions to gain more clarity. Be like a fascinated journalist who really wants an in-depth understanding.

**When the urge to interrupt arises, pause.** This takes some effort, but try to become aware of that moment when you want to butt in, and immediately reflect instead on whether your input is really necessary. Think about exactly what you're burning to jump in and share. Is it basically the same thing the other person is trying to say? Are you pre-empting a conclusion to their story? Bite your tongue and observe whether it really matters if *you* say it, or *they* do. If it still gets said and the conversation moves along enjoyably, then there's no real problem.

**Employ nonverbal cues like nodding, smiling, or making eye contact to express engagement without interrupting.** A certain level of engagement from you might convey to the speaker that you're listening closely and are being moved by their story. The trick is to make sure it always is *their* story—and not something you're picking up and making your own.

### How to Interrupt Properly

Keen-eyed readers may be wondering, "But what if the other person is rambling on and on? Unless I interrupt, I'll *never* get a word in edgewise!"

That's true. Sometimes we need to interrupt, but there is a way to do it while being polite and maintaining connection and rapport.

- Use phrases like "Excuse me" or "May I add something?" to indicate that you want to speak.
- Apologize for the interruption and acknowledge the speaker's thoughts before sharing your own.
- Wait for a natural pause in the conversation before interjecting.
- Use nonverbal communication like leaning in subtly, opening your mouth as though to speak, and using gestures like raising your hand or finger.

If you're talking to someone who seems to be suffering from extreme verbal diarrhea, then you may need to listen closely for a gap in the conversation and make your excuses.

## Don't Be a "Conversational Narcissist"

*In this chapter: Conversational narcissism is the tendency to center the self in conversation; a mindset shift is required to reorient toward what really matters—the other person.*

Have you ever felt totally exhausted after talking to someone? Maybe it was hard to put a finger on exactly why, but you felt extremely frustrated, even angry, as though you had just been trampled over somehow. This person may have given all the superficial indications that they were listening to you, and they may not have spoken any more in the interaction than you did. And yet, the whole thing still felt like it was all about them. Why? It's probably because they were a conversational narcissist!

Talking to a person like this always feels "off." They dominate and make everything about them, and even when they're listening, it only seems to ultimately serve them and the story they're telling. You may end up feeling subtly (or not-so-subtly) dismissed, invisible, or even a little crazy—as though nothing you said was really getting through. While they may have said all the right words, you may have left the interaction feeling that things were not quite as they seemed, and there was a lingering sense of distrust or confusion.

Now, here's the really difficult part to hear: There have probably been times in your life when you have made someone else feel this way. Though there are genuinely narcissistic people out there with pervasive patterns of selfish communication, the truth is that we *all* have the ability to focus a little too much on ourselves in social interactions.

Our conversation can be narcissistic even if we generally aren't narcissists ourselves. We are guilty any time we engage in a style of communication that consistently centers our own desires, needs, perspectives, and interests over everyone else's. The tricky thing is that this form of self-centeredness can be invisible—we can be conversational narcissists even while asking questions, making eye contact, and speaking less than the other person.

**See if you recognize any of these behaviors in yourself:**

- You interrupt often (we covered this in the previous chapter).
- You tell other people how you feel and what your opinion is, but are unsure of theirs (hint: it's possibly because you didn't ask them or you weren't listening when they told you).

- When someone tells you about XYZ, it reminds you of XYZ in your own life, and so you immediately share a story about XYZ. Except this story is more interesting because it's about you!
- You give unsolicited advice or think that the reason people are sharing a story with you is because they want to know what you think about it.
- You like being the center of attention, whether that's playing the entertainer, educating and informing people, or commanding the floor with your storytelling.
- You are quick to decide what you think about everything you're told—i.e., whether you agree or not, and what judgments you'll make about the various people and ideas involved. It's not that you evaluate people; it's just that you're really good at identifying inferior opinions . . .
- You often have an "agenda" when talking to someone and have a very definite idea of where the talk should be going.
- You may re-tell other people's stories or anecdotes as your own, or to make yourself look good.
- You occasionally *act* as though you're listening, but all the while you're thinking, "Wow, look at me go. I'm such an empath."

- You sometimes catch yourself bragging a little or bigging yourself up.

Granted, nobody likes to think that they're guilty of these behaviors, but the more honest we can be about our bad habits, the better chance we have of overcoming them. Conversational narcissism can play out in countless ways, but one thing that is always present is the **tendency to center the self**. What this means is that one way or another, the flow of conversational attention and energy is constantly being diverted toward one person and away from anyone or anything else.

Sometimes, the most narcissistic person in a conversation is actually not obvious. Watch where attention, energy, and focus are flowing, however, and you will always see it pointing toward the conversational narcissist. Family therapists, for example, often notice that in a group dynamic, it is not always the domineering father figure or the moody teenager who is controlling the family, but the unassuming grandma sitting quietly at the back. Though she doesn't speak much, when she does, it is always to turn the conversation back to herself and her interests.

This is to say that even if you consider yourself shy or self-effacing, you may still be using a narcissistic communication style if the effect of your behavior is to keep bringing attention back to yourself. This is a little like the person who complains at length about how unattractive they think they are, and yet somehow always finds themselves starting conversations where their appearance is the focus. Sometimes people can use kindness and compassion itself as a way to continually return attention to where they want it: themselves. Imagine you receive a gift from someone and then hear about it every day for a month afterward. "Remember when *I* got you that present you loved so much? That was so thoughtful of me, wasn't it? Man, I hunted for ages for that gift. Did I tell you the story?"

Overcoming conversational narcissism is simple but not always easy. It requires that we genuinely internalize the idea that we are not the center of every social interaction, *nor do we need to be*. The trouble is that narcissistic communicators often end up creating the exact kind of conditions that further trigger their narcissism. For example, because they never listen to people, people tend to tune them out or talk over them, leading to them feeling even more unheard and unappreciated . . . and therefore even more desperate to assert their superiority. It's a vicious cycle.

The only way to break out of that cycle is with a little humility. To oppose the narcissistic impulse, cultivate the opposite sentiment: that you are nothing special, that you may be mistaken or ignorant about something, that your opinions are not especially important or unique, and that the world is not waiting with bated breath to hear what those opinions are.

A narcissist may be surprised to find that rather than this sentiment being a catastrophe, it is actually a *relief* to not be the center of the universe. The big surprise is that so much anxiety and tension can be released once you realize that you do not need to prove yourself or convince anyone or get permission or validation from anyone. All you need to do is listen, be present, and be curious. How relaxing!

**Instead Of: Treating Others as Your Competition**
**Try: Taking Pleasure in Their Achievements**

A successful conversation involves cooperation and understanding rather than seeking attention or competing with others. Focus on learning from and listening to your conversation partner rather than trying to outdo them. If this is difficult, just remind yourself that being able to offer good-natured praise and recognition tends to make you look good, anyway!

## Instead Of: Planning and Rehearsing Your Response
## Try: Making a Fool of Yourself

It's not the end of the world to fumble a little with your words, to appear vulnerable for a moment in other people's eyes, to admit that you don't know the answer to a question, or to change your mind about something. When our ego is in charge, we make the mistake of thinking that if we're perfect, we'll win adoration from others; the opposite is usually true. It's when we are flawed and real and genuine that people can most identify with us.

## Instead Of: Giving Unsolicited Advice
## Try: Asking for Advice Yourself

Unsolicited advice is almost always self-serving and about the advice-giver's need to be recognized as wiser and more benevolent. If you notice the urge to make a pronouncement, turn it around by asking others for their unique insight and perspective. This will not only allow you to genuinely learn something new, but it will also engender trust and liking from the other person. "You're the expert on XYZ, aren't you? What do you think about all this?"

**Instead Of: Explaining Your Opinion**
**Try: Playing Dumb**

Conversations where two people agree on the best opinion and then congratulate themselves for having it are the most boring conversations! When it comes to current events or controversial topics, practice the fine art of *not* having an opinion. You don't always have to weigh in on everything. Be agnostic. Try stepping back and getting curious about other people's perspectives on things. Not only will this make you more interesting to talk to, but you may find that you yourself are more interested by the conversation that emerges . . .

**Instead Of: Oversharing**
**Try: Being a Little Mysterious**

People are seldom interested in things that are being actively forced down their throats, after all. Give people the time and space to *want* to get to know you, and have them invite you to share details of your life, rather than leading with too much information right off the bat. Keep a little of yourself in reserve.

## Listen Without Prejudice

*In this chapter: Letting our ego drive conversations means we often lead with prejudice, or pre-judgment. Instead, we can learn to encounter people as they really are (and that's often more interesting, anyway).*

When we speak about ego, what exactly are we talking about?

This is a concept with a long history and one that has evolved considerably over time. The ancient Greek philosophers had a related concept that encompassed an individual's total identity, and included their thoughts, feelings, actions, and character, bound together with notions of their virtues and vices.

At the turn of the century, Sigmund Freud introduced the term "ego," but it's psychological use was very different from our casual modern-day meaning. Freud's model was a psychodynamic one, meaning he understood the psyche of man in hydraulic terms. Across the different parts of the human's inner world, psychic energy could move around. Thus, for Freud there were conscious and unconscious regions (like known and unknown territories of a map), and furthermore a person was really several people in one: There was a primal and unconscious id down below, the regulating superego up above, and the ego playing the go-between somewhere in the middle. This ego was the part of the psyche that navigated the conflicting demands of the pleasure-seeking id and the ethical boundaries imposed by the superego. How well it managed told you a lot about the person's overall psychological health.

Today, this conception is outdated, although Freud's major concepts are now thoroughly embedded in our own thinking about the psyche. For example, most of us take for granted that there is such a thing as the "self," that there may be many components and parts to it, and that some of these parts may be unconscious. In modern usage, ego is not understood as the *self* but rather as *selfishness*. It's a term now associated with heightened self-esteem or self-importance, manifesting as arrogance, narcissism, or an inflated sense of one's abilities. While Freud's original meaning of ego was closer to our modern understanding of "self" or "self-concept," today we usually talk about ego when we really mean *big* ego.

In the Freudian sense, a healthy ego is one that is adapted to reality, mature, and stable. It's neither inflated nor shrunken. Too little sense of self and a person is weak, doubtful, ineffectual, and timid, but too much and they risk losing touch with reality, alienating others, and failing to learn from their mistakes. So, ego is not strictly the enemy. Rather, ego should remain in check and in proportion—it should ride in the back rather than steer from the driver's seat!

You'll know that ego is a problem when it starts to get in the way of connection, communication, and collaboration with others. Letting the ego rule means we bring a transactional, combative attitude to communication and end up becoming conversational narcissists who interrupt and dominate. Conversations become more about winning, asserting one's thoughts, and being heard instead of truly understanding the other person. You'll know that ego is a problem when you can't help continuously injecting your own stories into conversations, redirecting the focus back to yourself, "one-upping," or making comparisons. You may talk too much or always try to have "the last word."

But the ego can trip us up in unexpected ways too. Remember that a too-small ego can get in the way just as much as a too-big one can. If we are overly self-conscious, for example, we are automatically fixated on ourselves. It doesn't matter that our self-absorption comes from anxiety and self-loathing—we are still focused on ourselves, not the other person, and the end result is still a lack of listening. Any time we allow our own thoughts, feelings, and perspectives to dominate at the expense of being able to comprehend someone else's, then the ego is in charge. That may look like vanity and narcissism, or it may look like self-effacement, shyness, and victimhood—both pull you away from genuine connection outside of yourself.

Suspending your ego while listening is like opening a door to a richer and more meaningful connection with others. It's a conscious choice to set aside your own perspective, even if just for a moment, and truly immerse yourself in someone else's narrative. By doing so, you create a space where their words, emotions, and experiences can unfold without the interference of your own agenda.

Sometimes, it's easy to get caught up in the excitement of waiting for your turn to speak, formulating your response while missing the nuances of the other person's story. Most of us are so familiar with our own narratives that we genuinely do forget that they are narratives in the first place—it's like we are trapped in a closed room and don't notice the air becoming stale. We forget that there is a whole world outside that door, filled with millions of people who are not telling the stories we are and not seeing the world through the perspective we are. Even more startling, we need to realize that even though we are the center of our own universes, the same is true for everyone else: We are background characters in *their* world, where they are the main characters, and we are not. What's more, how they see us may have very little to do with how we see ourselves.

Bringing ego into conversation doesn't have to be as obvious as bragging or interrupting—most people are far more subtle than this. Being overly attached to your own perspective often looks like collecting other people's words and expressions and using them as building blocks to further construct your own narrative. It's continually choosing to view other people and their existence as mere tools to augment your own. People may not be able to consciously notice that you're doing this, but they will *feel* it.

For example, someone attends a party and falls ill, then decides to go home early. The hostess sees this and is concerned—but she is concerned because she thinks, "I wonder if they're mad at me? I wonder if everyone will think my party was bad?" The frame of reference is herself; she does not consider that the guest is inhabiting an entirely different world, one in which her and her party barely play a part. She does not pause long enough to imagine that the guest may be as self-absorbed in their own narrative as the hostess is by her own.

It is possible to listen to someone, to mentally comprehend the information they're sharing with you, to remember their birthdays, and so on, and yet *still* be largely egotistical in the way you engage with them. That's because as long as you are solely occupied with your own frame of reference and fail to consider theirs, *you are not actually engaging with them at all*, but with a picture you've made of them—a picture that is essentially a version of yourself. This is the difference between "I feel sorry for them; *I'd* hate to be in their shoes" and "I feel sorry for them; it must be hard for *them* to walk in their shoes right now."

Truly suspending your own ego is something that people think is easily done, but it really isn't. It takes practice and plenty of maturity and humility. Doing so, however, means you start to really appreciate the richness and depth of other people. It really is like discovering that there are seven billion universes out there, not just one. Understanding the lived experiences, feelings, and meaningful moments of a person who is not yourself is where true empathy flourishes. You not only open your ears but also your heart to the nuances of someone else's world. You become attuned to the subtleties of joy, pain, and everything in between. This deeper level of listening builds bridges between people, fostering a connection that goes beyond the surface.

What about **prejudice**, then?

Again, there are several layers of meaning hidden in this word. The everyday understanding is that prejudice is an unreasonable dislike of people from a particular ethnicity, group, or background, or a biased perception that isn't backed by experience.

But there is a deeper meaning—*prejudice means pre-judgment.* It's when we arrive at a conclusion about someone without gathering any genuine data about them or having a genuine interaction. It's coming to a verdict about who they are and what they mean without bothering to actually engage with them in any way first. Prejudice is usually understood to be a negative preconception about someone, but it can just as easily go the other way, too, and take the form of unfounded positive pre-judgments about a person simply because of the group they belong to.

Prejudice has strong implications to bigotry and discrimination, but in the context of being a better listener, it's a lot less serious than that: Having prejudice is essentially just laziness. If ever we think, "I know who this person is; therefore I already know what they're going to say, and I already know my opinion about what they haven't said yet," then you are in fact pre-judging them. This may be a self-fulfilling prophecy: Because you don't truly engage, you never give yourself the chance to learn that your assumptions about other people were incorrect. Here are some ideas for dropping your own prejudice:

## Put Yourself in Their Shoes . . . as Them, Not Yourself

Empathizing involves actively trying to understand the feelings and perspectives of others. For instance, if someone is expressing frustration at work, consider the challenges they might be facing. When responding, begin by acknowledging the emotions or experiences the other person has shared. For example, if someone expresses frustration, you could start by saying, "I can imagine that dealing with [specific challenge] must be really tough. Tell me more about how that's been for you."

Crucially, it's not about imagining what that person's situation feels like from your perspective, but what it might feel like from theirs. You might not find the work situation they're struggling with a big deal at all, but that shouldn't stop you from recognizing that it's difficult for *them*.

## Imagine Being Recorded

Sounds strange, but it works. Visualizing your words going down permanently on a recording device encourages more thoughtful communication. Imagine that everything you say is being recorded for others to hear— including people you're talking about who aren't in the room. This mental exercise helps you pause before speaking impulsively and choose words carefully.

## Put Your Opinions on Hold

Everyone has opinions. Yours may even be "right"! Being a good, unbiased listener doesn't mean you don't value anything or have any boundaries. It just means you understand how and when to set your own viewpoint aside and explore someone else's. Temporarily suspend belief in your own views and take up belief in theirs, just to see what it's like. What would it look and feel like to imagine that this person actually makes complete sense and that they have a good point? What might it be like to imagine a perspective that centers on this way of making meaning?

Initiate your response by expressing curiosity rather than immediately asserting your viewpoint. Start with phrases like "I'm interested in understanding more about your perspective on [topic]. Can you share more about why you see it that way?" Another trick is to simply postpone coming to any decisions. You don't have to have an opinion on everything, and even if you want to, you don't have to rush. Simply say, "Hm, that's interesting," and let it be for a moment.

### When THEY Are the Prejudiced One

Sometimes it's them, not you. If you're in the unfortunate position of having to interact with a person who has an oversized ego or a fixed idea of who you are before you've even opened your mouth, then you'll need a few more tools in your listening toolbox:

- Keep your cool. Remember that you can't control others, only yourself. Maintain a respectful and positive frame and know that no matter how rude or annoying someone is, they don't decide on how rude and annoying you *are*.

- Be crystal clear about your boundaries. Narcissistic people will take your open-ended question and your empathy and make you sorry you offered anything to them. Big-headed people need compassion and understanding as much as anyone, but you can choose how much you're willing to give before you draw a line in the sand.

- Be assertive but don't go into battle. Remember that to a big ego, everything is zero-sum, meaning there is always a winner and a loser. It's exhausting and pointless to compete with a person who feels psychologically unwilling to "lose"— i.e., cooperate with you. Know when to walk away, and don't take it personally— they certainly won't be!

- If someone has drastically underestimated you or cannot really see you because of the stereotypes they hold about who they think you are, well, let them. You cannot change them. Carry on being exactly who you are. You have nothing to prove, but your actions will always speak louder than words and may ultimately help loosen their fixed ideas.

- Finally, have a sense of humor about it. Remind yourself that you've also been a little stubborn, a little prideful, or a little narrow-minded in the past. Have empathy (from a distance) but don't worry too much about it. You don't have to see eye to eye with everyone all the time.

## Validating and Normalizing

*In this chapter: Empathetic and skillful listeners know the secret to good communication and being liked by others—it's simply to make others feel good.*

If we're guided by our egos, we're often chasing after one thing: We want confirmation from other people that what we think and feel makes sense, that we matter, and that people will acknowledge and value us because we belong. *All* human beings have this need, and it's a big part of why we communicate in the first place.

The irony is that many people feel so unseen and unheard that they resort to desperately trying to *win* attention by becoming conversational narcissists. It's ironic because by communicating this way, they actually ensure that other people listen to them even less and fail to give them the sense of care and validation they so badly want.

The only way out is to realize that it's your job to *offer* the other person the same thing that you are seeking from that interaction.

Most people crave validation without knowing what it really is. When we validate someone, we are not saying that we agree with them, that we like them, or that we are somehow granting them permission from a position of superiority. Validating doesn't mean explaining something or excusing it or praising it. When we validate someone and their perspective, all we are essentially saying is **you make sense**.

If something is valid, it has an internal logic and right to exist. It's legitimate and acceptable. It belongs in the world. Too often, however, we speak to others in a way that subtly communicates that their view is not really good enough, not right, not understandable, not acceptable, not likeable, and so on. We may send people the message that we don't genuinely respect their position and don't really believe that it has the right to exist, like our own. We may imply that their opinion is not understandable, or even that it's not worth trying to understand.

The major insight here is that you don't have to agree with someone in order to validate them. You just have to accept that they are as they are, and go from there. Think of how many arguments and disagreements would dissolve if both people truly felt that it wasn't necessary to resolve differences, only to *acknowledge* them and let them be!

Invalidation can creep in in many ways, even when we're trying our best to show empathy.

Someone may say, "I'm terrified," and a well-meaning friend may reply, "Terrified? Don't be silly, there's nothing to be afraid of!" It's a response that comes from a good place, but what it does is invalidate what is real for the first person: They *are* afraid. That's real for them. You may not agree that there is anything to be scared of, but being empathetic means seeing that their feeling of fear is valid nevertheless.

Normalization is a related concept and refers to treating other people's perspectives and experiences as normal, i.e., not judging or condemning them as strange or wrong. When we say, "It makes sense that you would feel scared in this situation. I'm sure most people would feel exactly the same way," you are normalizing the person's emotional response. You are validating them because you are confirming that they are not in fact crazy, and that their response to the situation is natural, expected, and reasonable. This makes people feel far less alone or misunderstood and paves the way for conflict resolution and real communication.

Here's how to validate people and normalize their experiences:

**Focus on the other person's emotions rather than your logic.** For example, if you're upset because you think the other person had unrealistic expectations for you to meet, and now *they're* upset because you didn't meet them, realize that you can have your emotions about the situation while still validating theirs with empathy.

Remember that their expectations come from their experiences, values, and beliefs (many of which may not have anything to do with you). You may believe that they expect certain things from you that you've made clear you can't carry out, but from their perspective, their expectations and disappointment are still valid.

In conflicts like this, it's easy to focus on your own experience and center it as more valid and more right than theirs. But remind yourself that they are in the exact same position as you—they feel that their position makes sense and that you're being unreasonable. Instead of saying, "It's not my fault you always expect me to XYZ! I've already told you I can't do it," you can say, "You have every right to be upset about this. I'm sorry you feel that way." Notice that you're not agreeing with them; you're simply acknowledging that they feel as they do, and they have a right to that feeling.

Once everyone feels that their position and their reactions are totally justified and acknowledged, *then* you can get to the business of resolving the issue at hand. If you fail to validate and normalize, however, you may be stuck going round in circles for a while.

**Add normalization to an apology.** Even if you're being blamed and are genuinely at fault, try not to become defensive. If you said or did something hurtful (intentionally or not), apologize and normalize as soon as possible. People may resist apologizing because they think it means admitting guilt and inferiority. Actually, it's the opposite—you are communicating that harmony and resolution are more important to you and that you're willing to do what it takes to move on.

Instead of saying, "I didn't mean to hurt you, so you really shouldn't be upset about this," you can say, "I'm sorry I said_____. I didn't mean to hurt your feelings, but I see how my words might have come off as offensive."

**Use validating and normalizing phrases.** It's not enough to have good intentions—try to make sure that you're communicating them loud and clear. Say things like:

"I can see why you'd feel that way."

"That makes sense."

"I'm not surprised you responded that way."

"I would think the same thing."

"It's completely normal."

**Use labels . . . without judgment.** It may sometimes help to put a name to what the other person is experiencing, but be careful that you're not putting words in their mouth or making subtle value judgments. Labeling works best when it attempts to put a name to an emotion or experience, but it's less helpful when it veers into diagnosing or covering up subtleties and nuances with jargon.

Good labeling: "Seems like you're feeling pretty overwhelmed right now."

Less-than-ideal labeling: "I bet you've got ADHD or something. Seems like everyone has it these days."

**Share your own experience . . . without comparing.** When emotions are running high, it's easy to feel like we are alone in our suffering or confusion. To hear that someone else has experienced the same issue that we're struggling with can be an enormous relief and helps validate and normalize in one go. If you have a relevant personal story to share, it may create trust and understanding. Be mindful, though, that you're not unconsciously trying to shift the conversation to yourself, give advice or subtly suggest what the right response is (i.e., yours). Finally, if you really cannot understand where someone is coming from, don't say, "I know how you feel." It may be more powerful for you to honestly admit, "Wow, I have no idea what that must feel like for you. I'm sorry." Keep listening, though, and you'll communicate that you're willing to learn more.

## Summary

- One of the biggest impediments to good listening and communication is the ego. Good communicators are secure, relaxed, humble, respectful, and curious, and see conversations as opportunities to learn, connect, and bond. They don't see difference of opinion as a threat and have no need to compete or convince.

- While the ego has its uses, don't let it get in the way of connection, communication, and collaboration with others. Put yourself in others' shoes, suspend judgment, and recognize that other people occupy different frames of reference.

- Interrupting people while they speak is actually a power play, usually driven by the ego. If you're an interrupter, be mindful of your habit and understand where it comes from, then commit to focusing more on people's words and showing support nonverbally and without interrupting.

- Conversational narcissism is the tendency to center the self in conversation. We are guilty any time we engage in a style of communication that consistently centers our own desires, needs, perspectives, and interests *over* everyone else's. Instead, give praise and take pleasure in other people's achievements, be comfortable with making a fool of yourself sometimes, ask for help and advice, and forego having or sharing an opinion.
- Everyone craves knowing that they matter, they make sense, they're valued and respected, and they belong. When listening, offer people this validation and verbally normalize their experience.

## Chapter 4: Curiosity Is King

### Stay CALM—with a Curious, Active-Listening Mindset

*In this chapter: The secret ingredient to next-level listening is a genuine interest—wonder, even—in what other people have to say.*

To listen well, we need to remove obstacles and noise, and especially get rid of our own egos. But then, what should take its place? That's easy: *curiosity*.

Curious active listening is an advanced form of active listening that emphasizes a genuine curiosity and a deep desire to understand the speaker on a profound level. It involves more than just hearing words; it requires being fully present in the moment, engaging with the speaker, and expressing a sincere interest in their thoughts and feelings. Who is this person in front of us, really? What are they actually trying to convey, on a deep level?

Curious active listening requires that we deliberately suspend our preconceptions, expectations, and judgments. It also requires that we temporarily set aside our own perspectives so there is space for *their* perspective to unfold. Granted, you don't need to learn to do this for every encounter with every random stranger you meet, but this mode of listening is an essential skill to develop for those situations where it's really needed.

Deep, curious listening enhances relationships in several surprising ways. First, it fosters empathy by enabling individuals to understand and connect with others on a more sincere emotional level. Trust, intimacy, harmony, and real connection are all boosted, and people begin to properly understand one another.

That means that not only are conflicts less likely, but should they arise, you are far better prepared to diffuse and resolve them. When both parties feel heard and understood through curious active listening, tensions diminish. The conversation can more quickly move on to finding solutions, rather than potentially generating more grievances.

Instead of wasting time and energy defending yourself or going into attack mode, you can quickly get on the same side and start working together on a way forward.

There's more, though. Learning to do this kind of listening brings personal benefits, too, including better patience, maturity, and creativity. Learning to pay attention and to read between the lines (for example, by noticing nonverbal communication more) and practicing the art of perspective-switching improves your mental and emotional agility and expands your horizons. It may seem strange, but learning to look at other people more closely can even expand your view to the extent that you are better able to understand yourself in the process. Good listeners, in other words, challenge both their hearts and minds to extend far beyond their ordinary limits, and the benefits are far-reaching.

According to *Agile Organization Development*, you can deliberately use CALM—a curious active-listening mindset—to help resolve conflicts, negotiate, and give and receive feedback in the workplace. Sharing feedback or airing grievances can be especially tricky since it usually activates people's egos and defensiveness. But once triggered this way, they instantly shut down and stop listening— which can quickly lead to stalemates, misunderstandings, or fresh conflict. Here's how active curiosity can diffuse all this:

## *Offering Feedback or Raising a Concern*

### Step 1: Make sure you're prepared

Don't just spring the issue on the other person, but rather introduce it gently or gradually. First make sure that you yourself understand what you wish to communicate and exactly what you're asking the other person to do. Raising an issue without any clear way forward may be more readily perceived as a complaint or criticism, so be sure you're ready to suggest a productive and realistic way forward.

Imagine that a colleague is frequently interrupting you during meetings, and you're starting to get annoyed. To start things off, you say something like, "Can I share with you something I've recently noticed?" or, "Can I talk to you for a moment about something that's on my mind?" You want to give the other person a heads-up so they don't feel like you've caught them off guard. You may have been stewing over an idea for days, but this may be the very first time they've heard of the issue, so don't rush into it.

### Step 2: Stick to the facts

Though it's tempting, don't lead with emotions (yours or theirs), but rather seek a more neutral common ground you can both agree on. This will naturally be the most objective facts of the situation at hand. Avoid blaming, labeling, making judgments, or offering interpretations, especially about the other person's character or motivations. Just state the facts in a way that the other person can easily agree with. Remember that people will be primed to feel attacked and want to defend themselves. Get around this by presenting a neutral and nonthreatening statement of fact that they can actively endorse.

In our example, saying, "You keep on interrupting me during meetings. Why do you have so little respect for me?" is leveling an attack that will only trigger defensiveness. Instead, say something like, "I've noticed for the last few weeks in our meetings that you will often start speaking before I've finished."

## Step 3: Check in with them

Once you've alerted them to the fact that you're sharing an issue with them and stated what you've observed, invite them to share their own thoughts with you. Doing this fairly soon in the conversation signals that you don't intend to lecture anyone but are interested in a genuine dialogue. With as much calm curiosity as you can muster, let go of your own assumptions and assessments of the situation and ask them what they think of what you've just shared.

Listen to understand, not to respond. Don't think or anticipate or prepare or interpret while you're listening. Just listen. You may say, "So I just wanted to check in with you and understand why that keeps happening. Any thoughts?" Then listen.

## Step 4: Paraphrase

Don't take it for granted that you understand right off the bat. Double-check by repeating in your own words what you've heard. You may like to literally say, "It sounds like XYZ . . . Have I understood that correctly?" If it's appropriate, acknowledge and thank them for their honesty.

In our example, the other person may express surprise and say they didn't even realize they were interrupting. They may explain that they are often very excited and inspired by what's being shared, and sometimes get a little anxious about not being heard, so they speak up to make sure they're not forgotten in the discussion. "Thank you for explaining that to me. That does help me understand things better. It sounds like you're not really aware you're interrupting, and you're not doing it on purpose, but rather you just get excited in meetings. Have I got that right?"

## Step 5: Express yourself

This is the important part. Only once you've laid the groundwork by stating the facts, and given them the chance to share their side of things, should you go ahead and express your view. State how you're feeling, what you've noticed, or any grievance you have, but use "I" language and focus on yourself. Then, respectfully ask for what you need to change or, if giving feedback, say what you need to say. For example, "The reason I bring this up is because being interrupted during a meeting is pretty frustrating for me, and it makes me feel as though my contribution is not being respected. Can I ask that you give me the space I need to talk during meetings in the future?"

## Step 6: Keep the door open

If the first few steps have been done well, the dialogue tends to resolve pretty quickly, with one or the other making a request for a change, and/or expressions of a wish to maintain the peace and continue to collaborate. In our example, the other person may simply need to have it pointed out that they were interrupting others during meetings, and since this wasn't their intention, they may themselves suggest they stay mindful of this habit in the future.

Wrapping things up, reiterate that you are always happy to communicate openly, thank them, and do whatever is appropriate to "keep the door open" and maintain a friendly atmosphere. "Thanks for speaking to me about this. I feel a lot better understanding what was going on. It's so important to me that our team communicates well, so I appreciate your honesty."

Now, the above example is obviously quite a small one, but the steps apply for more complex or emotionally charged issues, too. Just remember that the key ideas are:

- Do what you can to avoid triggering people's defensiveness by allowing them to prepare themselves. If the issue is a big one, you might like to schedule a chat in advance and give them the option to talk when they're ready.
- As soon as possible, ask them for their feedback and their perspective. Genuinely try to understand what things look like from their point of view *before* launching into your own.
- Even if you're upset and believe they're wrong or misguided, try to express your upset without blame, and try to

understand their point of view without railing against it or judging it.

### *Receiving Feedback or Hearing Someone Else's Concern*

Depending on the type of person you are, this may be more or less difficult! With a few adjustments, the same steps above can be applied to help smooth over those difficult conversations.

## Step 1: Listen with calm curiosity

As much as possible, try to suspend your desire to judge, interpret, or defend yourself, and just listen without any inward response. "Thanks for bringing this up. I'm all ears. Please go ahead."

## Step 2: Paraphrase

Remember that when you're reflecting what you've heard, don't sneak in any interpretation of your own. "If I understand you, you're saying that you feel I've been talking over you sometimes in our meetings, and it's making you feel a little disrespected. Seems like you're asking me to be a bit more mindful of not doing that so much in the future. Is that right?"

## Step 3: Acknowledge what you've been told

If someone has made a request or asked for something to change, try to explicitly acknowledge this, whether they're sharing a grievance with you or are providing some constructive feedback. "Thank you for sharing your thoughts with me. I appreciate that. It certainly is something I can work on, and I'll be doing my best to be aware of it in meetings from now on."

## Step 4: Ask for support

Someone might raise an issue with you without being very clear about what they expect from you now. If you're unsure about what to do with a piece of feedback, demonstrate that you're willing to collaborate by asking outright for help finding solutions. "I'm not always aware that I'm interrupting, so would you mind just politely reminding me in the moment if it happens again? Just saying something like 'I wasn't finished yet' might really help me break the habit. What do you think?"

Asking for solutions, suggestions, and opinions going forward is a great way to show that not only have you heard and acknowledged the problem, but you're committed to thinking of ways out of it.

## Step 5: Keep the door open

Even emotionally mature people can feel a little raw and vulnerable when receiving difficult feedback or being called out on something, but try to end the interaction as positively as possible. Express interest in maintaining harmony and collaboration going forward. Sometimes, especially if we feel attacked or picked on, we can subtly "punish" people for it by being overly aloof, formal, or "maliciously compliant." But you will be the bigger person if you can quickly get over your ego and turn your attention to maintaining good relations with the person in front of you.

"Well, I apologize again, and I'm grateful for the feedback, although it's a little hard to hear! I value your opinion, though, so please do speak to me anytime if something's on your mind. If you like, we can touch base in a few weeks after I've had a while to work on this. You can let me know how things are working for you."

This step may arguably be the most important. This is where you strongly signal that although there is some friction and tension, and although the conversation has been a little uncomfortable, ultimately the relationship will not be damaged. If you do it just right, you may even turn the episode to your advantage—your response to temporary friction may inspire more trust and rapport in the long run.

## Asking the Right Questions

*In this chapter: The purest expression of curiosity is a question. Pay attention to how, when, and why you ask them.*

One key aspect of effective listening involves the art of asking questions. But not just any old questions will do! A good question is one that stems directly from a genuine sense of curiosity. Without the pre-existing curiosity, your questions may stem instead from a personal agenda, from politeness, even from boredom.

So, what are the right questions to ask?

Annoyingly, the answer to this is a predictable "it depends."

The right question is one that best fits the unique conversation you're having in the moment, and which springs from your desire to understand more about the person in front of you. That said, there are some fundamentals that will make sure you're using questions to make the conversation flow, rather than come screeching to a halt.

## Tip 1: Ask open (but not too open!) questions

Closed questions are those that yield a "yes/no" or single-word response. They're easy for the other person to answer, but once they do, that's it. You're right back where you started unless the other person is gracious enough to supply you with more than you asked for. While closed questions do have their uses, open-ended questions are more conducive to fostering open and expansive discussions. It's a form of curiosity—you ask but with zero expectation of the kind of answer you may be given.

Beware, however, that a question can also be *too* open. Have you ever felt put on the spot by a question like "So what do you do for fun?" or "Where do you think you'll be in the next five years?" People may well have answers for these questions, but they're usually not at the ready and are often too big to be answered gracefully. You may inadvertently put a lot of pressure on someone to come up with a good answer, straining the conversation. Instead, aim for somewhere in the middle. "Do you picture yourself continuing to live in LA for the next couple years?"

## Tip 2: Avoid asking "why" questions

While this may seem like a great way to really dig into the details, the why question can make people feel appraised or judged or as though you're asking them to explain or justify themselves to you. You may be asking out of genuine curiosity, but it may come across as nosy or like an interrogation. "Why did you move to LA?" sounds a little accusatory, while "What do you think made you choose LA as your next big move?" sounds a lot kinder.

## Tip 3: Use softening language

Technically, a question is asked with who, where, what, why, and so on, but you can also ask a question obliquely.

> "I'm wondering whether . . .?"

> "Is it possible that . . .?"

> "Can I ask about . . .?"

This kind of indirect language serves two main purposes: It poses a question in a nonthreatening way, which may be useful during a conflict or a high-stakes situation, but it also shows politeness and tact more generally.

## Tip 4: Keep things balanced

Try to avoid asking too many questions in a row. Stick to two or three at an absolute maximum, but try to vary the pattern of back-and-forth in the dialogue so that it doesn't resemble an interview. Sometimes, socially anxious people may use questions as a form of defense. As long as the other person is in the spotlight, so to speak, they can retreat a little.

This will lead, however, to a one-sided conversation pretty quickly and might frustrate the other person. Mix up your questions with statements, expressive responses, and a little something about yourself so it doesn't feel as though you are demanding that the other person open up without being willing to do so yourself.

## Tip 5: Let your questions build

The best way to show that you are paying attention and care about what you're hearing is to tailor questions to the conversation as it unfolds. Let each question be a meaningful response to the previous answer, and remember what you're told so you can feed that back in the form of a thoughtful follow-up question that really means something.

## Tip 6: Avoid loaded questions

Any time you ask a question, you are narrowing the field of possible answers you're willing to receive. Not only does this steer the conversation, but it also frames the other person's response in a particular and unneutral way. To understand this point about narrowing the field of potential answers, simply consider the question "Have you stopped mugging little old ladies yet?" and how meager your available responses are!

A loaded question is one that forces an answer, or one that comes with its own built-in assumptions, expectations, and judgments. You may be asking someone a question, but you are actually telling them about your own values and preconceptions. Take a look at the implied statement loaded into these questions:

"How are you going to apologize?" (Implication: you are going to apologize.)

"Is your home security system needing an upgrade?" (Implication: you have a home security system, or at least you *should* have one.)

"Are you staying for dinner or are you just going to abandon us?" (Emotionally loaded!)

"You're not serious about taking that job, right?" (Is this a question or is it really a statement in disguise?)

"Do you find it difficult to hide your incompetence at work?" (Not just one assumption, but two!)

### *Questions to Avoid at all Costs*
It's a good rule of thumb that if you're unsure what to say, ask a question. There are definitely some questions, however, that should be avoided for all people in all circumstances. Though these might seem

pretty obvious when listed out below, the fact is that they can skirt some more conventionally acceptable questions, so it's easy to accidentally put a foot wrong and say something you regret.

In general, avoid asking questions about:

## People's Reproductive or Parenting Choices

"So, when are you guys having kids/more kids?"

"Why don't you try IVF/adoption/getting a dog?"

"Why aren't you trying to breastfeed?"

## How Much People Earn, Spend, or Owe

"How much are they paying you?"

"How much did you pay for your house?"

"When are you planning to retire?"

"Does your wife earn any income?"

"Will you inherit anything from your grandparents?"

## People's Sex Lives and Relationship Status

"When is he going to pop the question?"

"How's your ex doing these days?"

"Are you gay?"

"Why are you still single?"

## People's Appearance, Weight, or Eating Habits/Choices

"Why don't you eat meat?"

"Have you lost/gained weight?"

"You look different. Have you had work done?"

"Are you on a diet?"

It's also a good idea to avoid probing questions about people's religious beliefs, political orientation, health issues, legal troubles, family conflicts, educational background, or current job status. It's not that you can never talk about these things (they're often the most interesting and important things!). It's just that it's best to wait until the other person volunteers that information, rather than going hunting for it yourself.

Pay close attention to their nonverbal communication, and if you suspect you've touched a nerve, respect that boundary by immediately changing the topic. Good intentions won't matter much if you accidentally cause offense, and you can never really be sure what someone is experiencing or what their perspective on a situation is.

## Listening to Nonverbal Cues

*In this chapter: When you listen to what a person is saying, listen to EVERYTHING they're saying . . .*

Let's take a closer look at nonverbal communication and how it can make a world of difference in a conversation. Staying curious, open-minded, and receptive is a great way to connect more deeply to others, but small changes in our body language or voice can quickly change "curious" to "nosy" or even "demanding." Context is everything.

Imagine, for example, that someone asks you the following question: "So, where did you go to college?"

On its own, this question is fairly innocuous. If someone asked you this question after you were describing the degree you've just completed, and as they did so they had a relaxed, smiling face and a gentle intonation, you'd rightly assume that they were simply curious, paying attention, and following the natural flow of the conversation. But now imagine that someone asks this same question verbatim, but with an ever-so-slightly sarcastic tone, while faintly frowning and looking as though they were amused or confused. Imagine them asking this question immediately after you apologize for mispronouncing a French word at a restaurant. Picture them saying, "So, where did you go to college?" while they tilt their head to the side and quickly look you up and down. You get the picture: same words, *very* different meaning.

Nonverbal communication is constantly flowing back and forth between people—what varies is the degree to which we are paying attention to this information. Good communicators naturally pay attention to the messages they're broadcasting with their own body language, but they're also experts at noticing other people's body language. Effective listening goes beyond words and absorbs information that cannot be obtained through verbal communication alone.

Nonverbal cues include:

- Body language—how close someone is standing to you, their posture, their overall physical demeanor, their gestures, and their facial expressions.
- Their voice—how loud or quiet, how fast or slow they're speaking, whether their voice is monotone or highly dynamic and changing, whether they're breathless or

controlled and even, the quality of the voice (is it warm, lyrical, staccato, crisp, husky?), and the pitch (high or low) .

- Formality of expression—are people being casual or formal, are they using slang or swearing, are they speaking in an official and neutral way or more colorfully and poetically? Also, how and when are they using silence? Why?
- Clothing and appearance—what do someone's clothing, accessories, footwear, etc. reveal about their identity and what they most wish to convey to others?
- Context—where and when is this conversation taking place? Is the person congruent with their surroundings or notably different in some way? What does the difference tell you about them?
- Gestures and movement—is someone "closed" and hunched in, or are they taking up a lot of room, moving quickly, and gesturing with lots of animation? Where is their eye contact (and therefore their attention) focused on?
- Finally, discrepancies—how is all this information coming together (or not)? Does the verbal message clash somehow with the nonverbal? Is there a tension somewhere? Be curious about what this means (more on this in the next chapter).

All the above can provide additional layers of meaning to a conversation. In fact, nonverbal communication may contribute *more* to your understanding of the speaker's message than their words alone.

Nonverbal cues, including "discourse markers" in spoken language and other nonverbal expressions, are rich sources of information. These cues help structure and annotate speech content, providing context and nuances that may not be explicitly stated.

Daniel Goleman, author of *Emotional Intelligence*, emphasizes the importance of nonverbal cues in the context of attention. He suggests that a constant flow of nonverbal exchanges occurs in every interaction—if only we're prepared to pay attention to it. Listening well, then, is not just a matter of paying full attention and listening with targeted, nonjudgmental awareness; in a way it's also about expanding your awareness to include other potential observations. Good listening is thus not just about empathy and attention, but also about being able to take in all the many aspects of a social situation and synthesize them into a coherent whole.

People who can do this well may sometimes be felt by others to almost be mind readers, but there is no magic involved! Simply looking at what is right in front of you is the only skill required. People are unable to do this primarily because:

- They've made some premature assumptions about what the conversation is and so don't feel they need to pay that much attention.
- They're genuinely not interested.
- They're interested, but their attention is divided, with much of it turned inward as they entertain their own thoughts and prepare responses to what they're hearing.
- They're anxious and too focused on themselves, i.e., they can't properly focus on others because they're self-consciously focusing on themselves instead.

Focused attention, open-mindedness, and emotional intelligence all come together and help you get the most out of your interactions with other people. Try to remember that **you are your message**, and the opposite is true as well: Other people are their messages. Listen to their words, yes, but try also to read *them* as people—their message will suddenly become much richer and three-dimensional.

According to Professor Michael Higdon, nonverbal channels surpass verbal communication in two ways: They carry more information and are believed more. Nonverbal cues encompass a broad range, including body movements, voice characteristics, spatial features, temporal aspects, and environmental factors. These cues provide a wealth of information that can be more influential and persuasive than verbal communication.

The reason for this is that nonverbal or embodied communication is assumed to be primary. Even babies cannot help but express their reality through their facial expressions and gestures. Deception and concealment, however, is easier when done verbally. If people are faced with a person whose words are saying one thing while their body is saying another, they tend to assume that the body is telling the truth. Body language is always spontaneous, hard to fake, and difficult to hide or manipulate.

Many professionals are only able to do their work when they learn to properly "listen" to body language. Lawyers listen carefully to what's *not* said and pay attention to clues of potential deception and what people may be really expressing in more circuitous ways. Similarly, doctors, counselors, teachers, carers, and service providers of all kinds are best at their work when they can "read between the lines."

Unless you never work with human beings in any capacity, it's likely that paying attention to nonverbal cues will be essential for doing your work, too. Understanding these cues allows for a deeper comprehension of people's needs, concerns, and emotions. Listening to how people express themselves tells you how they think, what they want and need, what they value, and why they're communicating with you. Listening carefully to everything that a person expresses helps you draw good boundaries, tailor your own communication, and avoid conflict.

With this in mind, the next time you're listening to a close friend or family member, talk about what's going on in their lives. Don't only listen to their words. Instead, imagine your awareness opening up and allowing in *everything* they are currently expressing. First and foremost, consider their bodies.

In a broad sense, what is their body as a whole communicating? Is it advancing or retreating, is it getting bigger or smaller, is it static or dynamic? If their body could *say* something, what would it be saying? The face and voice are also a part of the body—what are they doing? The voice, the breath, the emotions, and the verbal expression are all connected. For example, a person who is scared and tense will breathe in a more constricted and shallow way. You can hear this constriction in their voice, which will sound more choked, thinner, and quieter, but you can also see it everywhere else in the body, which may be hunched over as though in protection.

None of these observations on their own tell you that the person is scared, however; rather, it's all of them together that paint a coherent picture. The complete picture is a message of fear and protection. And if the person is saying, "I'm okay, really. Please don't worry about me," then you have loads of additional information: The person seems scared yet does not want to say so. Why? Context will likely tell you. Does this person feel that you might judge them if you know how scared they are? Do they feel interrogated? In context with all their nonverbal communication, their verbal expression "don't worry about me" takes on a richer meaning: They are telling you that they are also afraid of sharing their true feelings with you, or that they don't want to draw attention to themselves.

Even though the above observations may only take a few seconds to notice, they will allow you to instantly see a good way forward with this person: To defuse their fear, clearly communicate that you will not be judgmental and that you are not a threat. This means that it's probably a bad idea to keep pushing them to open up or force a hug on them! Instead, adapt your own communication style so that all your nonverbal and verbal expression sends the message: *I'm not judging you. I'm not a threat. I'm here to genuinely help you*.

Perhaps you take a small step back to give them space, turn your body slightly away from them, and relax. You smile, take a deep breath, slow your voice, and speak in a lower, gentler pitch. You may say, "Oh, of course, I understand. It's just that you seem a little on edge. I hope you'll let me know if you want to talk . . . I'm always here." Then you may change the topic to something amusing and light-hearted. If the literal conversation between you were transcribed word for word, it wouldn't look like much. But the truth is that you and this person have "talked" very effectively. They have said, "Look, I'm not ready to communicate about it right now. I'm pretty nervous and scared about what you'll think of me," and you communicated back, "That's okay. I won't push you. But I'm here and I care."

All of this was not done via words, but through nonjudgmental presence, "listening" to body language, understanding the other person's perspective and message, and responding to it in an appropriate and empathetic way. Doing the same in your own conversations is simple:

**Step 1:** Pay attention to nonverbal cues and the bigger picture they're painting.

**Step 2:** Tentatively share your observations—for example, by saying what you think *seems* to be happening (e.g., "You seem a little on edge . . .". This provisional labeling gives them a chance to respond and react, while signaling your willingness to be corrected.

**Step 3:** Adjust your nonverbal cues accordingly. If you want to support someone's negative emotion, you might counter theirs—for example, by communicating calm and relaxation while they're clearly experiencing tension and fear. On the other hand, if you want to show support for their positive emotion, you may mirror them and match their expression. If they raise the pitch and speed of their voice, you may do the same.

**Step 4:** Think about what they need. People communicate because they're trying to get their needs met. Once you can identify how a person is feeling and the overall message they're conveying, try to understand what they most want you to know and what need they currently have unmet. In our example, the need may be for privacy, for gentleness, and for people to not "make a big deal" out of their experience. The trick, of course, is to see and acknowledge their need even if it's not yours. This focus on their needs will naturally make you more attuned and empathetic. For example, say, "You seem frustrated. Are you okay?" rather than, "Why are you so angry at me?"

**Step 5:** Meet that need as best you can. Think about how you can talk so they can hear, and what actions you can take to signal that you've heard and acknowledged their position. What's "right" depends entirely on the unique situation. You may need to offer reassurance, clarity, more listening, silence, encouragement, or even a little pushback. If you've listened well, you're in the best position to know what your next step should be.

## Listening to Spot Lies

*In this chapter: Listen carefully to how people use language, and you can learn to more easily spot deception.*

Listening closely means we are better equipped to understand people, meet their needs, and connect with them on a deeper level. But one interesting side effect of becoming a better listener is the ability to perceive deception. Though this is a skill that can obviously come in handy throughout life, it's not just about spitting at someone who is lying to you—it's about noticing all the many ways that people use concealment and "massage the truth" for their own ends. Learning to see past this kind of subtle manipulation opens a whole new world to your comprehension.

First, the bad news: most people vastly overestimate how good they are at spotting lies, often because there are so many myths and misconceptions around how to spot a liar. A comprehensive review published in *Psychological Science and Public Interest* by Aldert Vrij found that the more that participants reported using visual and behavioral cues to spot a liar, the worse they performed. This suggests that things like watching where a person looks or whether they fidget or demonstrate another "tell" won't help you spot a liar.

What *does* work, however, is listening to the language of the potential lie and how it's being delivered. The new advice for spotting a liar is to focus on listening rather than visual cues, emphasizing the importance of language nuances and contradictions in detecting deception. To identify a liar, the key is attentive listening, as false stories demand more imagination and differ in language from truthful narratives. Examining word choices and grammar can reveal hidden meanings. The case of Susan Smith, who falsely claimed her children were kidnapped, illustrates this. Her unusual use of language in her story exposed her deception, leading to a later confession that she had drowned her children.

In 2015 Judee Burgoon and her research team conducted a close linguistic analysis of a thousand statements made by CEOs and CFOs who were eventually proven to be fraudsters. They noticed predictable patterns. These patterns emerge because, essentially, lying is hard work—it takes more mental energy and effort than simply telling the truth. To catch a lie, then, you need to listen closely for signs of this additional cognitive load. Says Burgoon:

"Because of the increased cognitive load and the human mind's finite processing capacity, liars will have difficulty simultaneously maintaining a false story and producing linguistically complex utterances. In other words, the more difficult it is for deceivers to concoct a believable response, the more they must resort to simpler language."

This simpler language may look like:

- Keeping statements quite short
- Using "fuzzy" hedging language (e.g., "I guess," "maybe," "could have been")
- Distancing language that puts space between the liar and the lie (e.g., avoiding first-person language like "I" and "me" and using passive forms like "the money was lost" instead of "I lost the money")
- More positive rather than negative emotion words, possibly to put a positive spin on things

The study also revealed something the researchers didn't predict, however: that the fraudulent statements tended to be longer and more complicated than those made by people known to be telling the truth. So, which is it?

Try to put yourself in the shoes of a liar. Your task is to use your imagination to describe a sequence of events that didn't actually happen, but do it in such a way that it appears genuine. To tell a lie, then, you need to *imagine* what that situation would be like if it had really happened. You may be a great liar if your imagination is excellent, but more often than not, people reveal that they have made this leap of imagination by the language they use.

Recall Susan Smith, who told reporters with tears in her eyes, "My children wanted me. They needed me. And now I can't help them." Susan had imagined a story where her children had been kidnapped, and was trying to convince others that this conjured-up story was true. Her imagined story, however, wasn't complete—by using the past tense, she accidentally told the *real* story, i.e., that her children were already dead, and she knew it.

A person may reveal a lie by saying too much, by saying too little, and by saying things in an unexpected or contradictory way. Someone who is suddenly going to great lengths to make up a detailed story may be "protesting too much" and literally making up the lie on the spot. On the other hand, a person who keeps repeating the same simple statement over and over again could be trying to conceal the fact that they can't keep up mentally with their own lie and are keeping quiet for fear that they'll say something incriminating.

If you're someone who wants to get good at detecting lies, it's a question not of noticing certain "telltale" behaviors or language choices, but noticing *how these choices fit into the rest of the context* and how they might be serving that person. Linguistic complexity could mean a lie, or it could mean the truth; the difference is made in the context. Here are some tips for lie-spotting that will genuinely work:

**Be Patient**

Think about the last time you discovered you'd been lied to. Recall what the lie was about, how it was told, why you believed it, and how you discovered it was a lie. Importantly, how long did it take you to spot the deception?

Chances are, you learned of the lie quite a while after it was told, and the deception was discovered because new information came to light, either from physical evidence or a third party. Some estimates say that just four percent of lies are detected within the hour they're told, with the bulk of lies being uncovered within a month or so. This is important: It means that catching a liar in the act is unlikely. Instead, be patient and let evidence accumulate. Many people can deceive for a little while—but not forever.

**Pay Attention to Linguistic Complexity**

You are not looking for increased or decreased complexity per se; rather, you're looking for evidence of increased cognitive *effort*. Some people may attempt to conceal this effort by speaking in overly simple terms. Others may do so by indulging in linguistically complex stories. What you need to pay attention to is how linguistic complexity is changing over time. If the person is ordinarily quite straightforward but suddenly falls over themselves telling you a very detailed story, ask why. Similarly, watch out for someone who is ordinarily relaxed and chatty, but suddenly clams up and gives you a simple, detached, and repetitive story. Notice if people suddenly seem to be thinking a lot. This may look like tension, distraction, or concentration.

## Observe Speech Patterns

Analyze the structure of statements, looking for signs of wanting to gain psychological distance from the lie. Notice first-person-pronoun use like *I*, *my*, and *me*. "I think you did so well today" is more likely to signal sincere praise than "Looks like the judges liked your presentation." If people are falsely reporting a stolen car, they are more likely to say "*the* car" rather than "*my* car." Finally, think about how someone may be using words like *we* or *us*, which signal psychological association. Someone may say, "We got in the car," when the story is about a romantic date night, but, "He put me in the car," if telling a tale of criminal abduction. If someone is talking about criminal abduction but saying, "We got in the car," this may raise a subtle red flag since it signals a kind of association or cooperation that doesn't fit in with the story.

## Look for Inconsistency and "Fuzziness"

Often, a lie is discovered purely because it is internally incoherent, i.e., it trips itself up. Fraudulent statements may exhibit a lack of clarity, including more hedge words, distancing language, and uncertain statements. But they also may exhibit a certain convolutedness that isn't generally present in truthful stories. It's here that a liar may reveal that their story doesn't quite add up. One obvious technique is just to encourage the person to keep talking until they make a mistake. Another is to listen for what may be deliberate fuzziness—i.e., the person doesn't want to commit themselves to any claim and so is actively setting up statements they can later plausibly deny if caught.

## Look Out for Overcompensation

If people are trying to give a certain false impression, they may overact, so to speak, and go too far. A person bluffing that they have a good hand in poker, for example, often jumps in to make their exaggerated claim, when in reality, a person with a good hand would more likely downplay how good it is. So, watch for people giving too much effort and energy to a performance. Note if a person immediately starts defending their story even when it hasn't been questioned yet, or starts providing evidence that wasn't asked for.

Ralph Waldo Emerson once said, "People do not seem to realize that their opinion of the world is also a confession of character." This is a great thing to keep in mind when trying to uncover people's lies or subtle deceptions. When telling an untruth, a person is at liberty to create any story they like. The story they do choose to tell will often reveal a lot about how they see themselves, the world, and their place in it. Our fabrications can't help but be colored by our own perceptions. Ask yourself if the story you're being told is something you'd expect more from this particular person; is it colored by their own feelings, expectations, and values?

Spotting lies is tricky work. Being a good listener, however, will always come in handy since it will allow you to spot all those other, more nuanced deceits and white lies we all engage in from time to time. The more you listen, the better you'll be able to notice when people are telling you what they think you want to hear, when they're holding something back, when they're embellishing the truth, or when they're being deliberately evasive. Lies are a human technology that we acquired when we learned to use language; understand exactly how other people use that language, and you instantly understand how they might lie.

## Summary

- A curious active-listening mindset (CALM) is about genuine curiosity and a deep desire to understand the speaker on a profound level. It requires the suspension of our own perspective, preconceptions, expectations, and judgments so we can encounter theirs. CALM is especially useful for conflict resolution, addressing grievances and issues, negotiation, and giving and receiving feedback in the workplace.
- Be prepared, stick to the facts, paraphrase what you hear, and check to see that you've properly understood. Listen to understand, not to respond. Express yourself respectfully and prioritize collaboration

and connection. Calm curiosity diffuses defensiveness and misunderstandings.

- Questions are great, but ask the right ones. Choose thoughtful, polite, exploratory open-ended questions that aren't loaded or delivered as an interrogation. Let them build meaningfully to show genuine interest. Avoid questions about money, people's romantic lives, appearance, and so on.
- Nonverbal communication (voice, body language, appearance, etc.) is just as, if not more so, important as verbal communication. Pay attention to a person's total expression, and reflect this back in your own communication.
- Listen well and you can spot lies more easily; pay attention to the way people use language, and forget about using visual or behavioral cues. Listen closely for inconsistency, hedging, fuzziness, odd use of pronouns, overcompensation, distanced language, and evidence of an increased cognitive load.

# Chapter 5: Communication and Conflict

## Emotional Self-Regulation

*In this chapter: The best way to avoid getting into conflict with people is to first learn how to make peace with YOURSELF.*

When people experience intense emotions like anger, frustration, or anxiety, their bodies initiate a stress response marked by heightened production of stress hormones, leading to increased heart rate, blood pressure, temperature, and breathing rate. These physiological changes often manifest as a short temper, emotional outbursts, mood swings, and a general influx of negative emotions.

The implication is clear: **If you are not in control of your emotions, they're often in control of you**. In everyday encounters, emotional dysregulation is the single greatest threat to communication—whether the dysregulation is theirs or yours. Imagine a "Chinese finger puzzle," those little devices where a finger is trapped in each end of a small tube. If you are overcome by your personal experience of stress at being trapped in such a puzzle, you will waste time struggling and resisting. It's only when you can suspend your automatic emotional reaction long enough to notice what's going on that you can start to form a strategy to get out of the trap. You do something counterintuitive—push your fingers together rather than continue to yank them apart—and you are instantly released from the trap. Human communication is similar: When either party is trapped in their own knee-jerk emotional response, they are unable to respond in a conscious, deliberate way.

To get out of the communication "finger puzzle" requires that we stop struggling, and gain a little distance from our automatic emotional responses. Proficient practitioners of emotional self-regulation have the ability to identify emotional triggers, assess potential consequences of responses, and intentionally choose actions that contribute to positive outcomes. Conversely, individuals lacking in this skill may display tendencies such as overreacting to situations, quick-trigger emotional outbursts, prolonged negative emotional states, and pronounced mood swings—i.e., all the things that are likely to trap them even tighter!

In this chapter, we're discussing conflict resolution. We won't begin, however, by looking at other people or what they're doing or how we might communicate so as to better influence them. Rather, we'll begin with *ourselves*. The better we are personally able to regulate our emotions, the better we can communicate. As a happy side effect, improved self-regulation means we're better able to recognize when other people are overcome by their emotions, and how best to deal with it.

In emotional situations, effective communication becomes crucial, requiring not only active listening but also understanding. While the natural instinct may be to focus on expressing personal thoughts and feelings, true communication involves considering the other person's perspective. The intensity of one's own emotions may interfere with clearly hearing the other person's words and grasping their underlying feelings; this results in miscommunication and relationship breakdowns.

Emotional regulation rests on a few fundamentals:

- We are not our emotions; we are just experiencing our emotions.
- Emotions are never pervasive, personal, or persistent, meaning that how we feel right now about something doesn't apply to everything, for all time, and it isn't something to take personally.
- The only way to manage emotions is to be **aware** that we're having them in the first place.
- Our emotions are always valid, but they may not be "true," i.e., just because we feel guilty or attacked or right, it doesn't mean we actually are.
- Other people cannot *make* us feel one way or another; similarly, our feelings don't compel other people to respond in any particular way or to feel the same.

Learn to work *with* your emotions and you are able to retain your autonomy and awareness in any situation, no matter how difficult. Work *from* your emotions, however, and you risk creating more trouble for yourself. To make this distinction clear: working from your emotion of anger may mean lashing out in a rage at someone and hurting their feelings. Working with your anger may mean thinking, "I'm too mad to talk right now. I need to call a time-out before I say something I regret," and removing yourself from a triggering situation.

Similarly, working from a feeling of hurt and betrayal may mean that you interpret everything the other person says as an insult targeted directly toward you. If you are aware of yourself having a feeling of hurt and betrayal, however, you can locate this experience within yourself and not project it onto the other person. You're then able to own that feeling, set it aside, and make efforts to hear what the other person is *actually* trying to tell you.

The moment you are aware of a potential conflict arising, **stop**. Just pause for a moment and become aware of how your emotions may be influencing your perceptions and ability to listen to the other person. Also become aware of how their emotions may be potentially influencing them and their ability to communicate in turn with you:

1. **Pay special attention to evidence of strong emotions, both in yourself and in the other person.** This is where

you tune into your own body or read the nonverbal communication of the other person. Is there a sudden change in tension, discomfort, alertness, confusion? Pay attention and you may notice that first little "snag" where things sour or a rupture occurs.

2. **Slow right down.** Sometimes at the first inkling that a conflict has arisen, people may anxiously try to avoid or quickly rush past the issue. They may start to ramble to fill in an awkward silence, or raise their voices in an attempt to regain control over things. But while the impulse may be to do something, anything, try instead to slow down or stop entirely. Take a deep, slow breath. Consciously feel your body and choose to release any tensions you become aware of—often in the neck, shoulders, and jaw. Soften your overall body posture, and if you speak, lower your voice both in pitch and volume.

3. **Try to find a little distance.** When you're overcome with emotion, it means you have become fused with it. To *de*fuse, you need a little psychological space between you and what you're experiencing. Give a name to your emotion or theirs (or both). If

possible, gain some temporal or spatial distance by asking for alone time or to have the discussion at a later time so you can process and gain perspective.

4. **Respect your own emotions.** Emotional self-regulation doesn't mean you deny what you feel or try to control it or make it something else. Whether it's before, during, or after a difficult conversation or conflict, fully acknowledge how you feel and give yourself time to process. You might like to write in a journal to help you work through things, or else chat to a neutral third party to clarify your thoughts and feelings. Having strong emotions is not good or bad in itself. What you do with them, however, matters.

5. **Challenge your assumptions and biases.** Once you've acknowledged and owned your feelings, you can set them aside for a moment and attempt to think through the conflict in a more strategic way. Take a fresh look at some of your knee-jerk responses. Is it true that the other person is deliberately trying to hurt or offend you? Is it possible that you are being unreasonable in some small way? What does the whole story look like from their perspective? Is there anything

that you have in common in this situation? Thinking this way can directly lead you to start imagining ways out of the conflict and toward a solution that works for both of you.

Sometimes, all that is required is that we make enough space between our emotions and our actions. Try always to address and understand your own emotional reaction before saying something or making your next move. This way, you are *responding* and not merely *reacting*. Finally, one thing to bear in mind is that even if you don't get any of this right, it's not the end of the world. Losing your temper or saying something inflammatory in the heat of the moment happens to all of us now and then. You may only become aware of your emotions once they're in full swing, but that's okay—better late than never! Gain composure as soon as you can and apologize so you quickly set the stage for something better. There's nothing wrong with saying something like, "Hey, I'm sorry for snapping at you earlier. I didn't mean it, but I understand it wasn't fair to you. Can we try again?" If someone else deals with their own emotions a little inelegantly, try to muster as much compassion and patience with them. Rather than pounce on their outburst, be quick to forgive and move on.

## Four Types of Responses

*In this chapter: Listening is not just about being there to support people who are angry or sad; it's also about knowing how to handle people's joy and excitement.*

When most people think of conflict, they imagine an outright argument or disagreement. Actually, there are many tinier, more subtle ways that the connection between people can rupture. How we react and respond to someone's negative emotions is certainly a worthwhile skill to master, but it may be that the way we respond to their positive emotions is just as important.

In his lecture on positive psychology, Martin Seligman identifies four distinct types of responses to someone's positive news, each with implications for the quality of that connection. The principle is fairly obvious: When someone is expressing something to us, we best show our comprehension and acknowledgement of that feeling by *mirroring* it ourselves.

Responses can be either active or passive and constructive or destructive (meaning, they either build up or break down the connection between two people). Take a look at the following four response types, each with an example for how someone might respond to a common situation: someone telling them the news of their recent engagement to the love of their life.

1. **Passive–Constructive Responding (being a buzzkill):** Passive–constructive responding is characterized by a positive acknowledgment, but one that lacks enthusiasm or genuine engagement. An example might be saying, in a kind of distracted way, "Aw, isn't that nice? Congrats." While the sentiment is positive, the response is passive and may not contribute significantly to the emotional connection between partners. The primary emotion is not being reflected back, and the person sharing the news will probably feel unsupported and unacknowledged (although, since it's technically a good response, they may not be able to say exactly why they're upset, or raise any objection).

2. **Passive–Destructive Responding (dismissing or one-upping):** Passive–destructive responding involves the same lack of genuine interest or acknowledgment, but it's worse since it doesn't even offer a nominally positive

response. So, someone says, "I'm engaged!" and they respond, "Oh. What's for dinner?" This response illustrates indifference; there will be plenty of hurt caused, but it is done so passively. It's as though the person is communicating, "I don't share your emotion, and what's more I don't care about it and it's not important." Another possibility is one-upping the person to bump them out of the spotlight and put yourself there instead: "You're engaged? I've been engaged for months."

3. **Active–Destructive Responding (nitpicking, finding problems, and criticizing):** One step worse than a passive–destructive response is one that is destructive in a more active and deliberate way. Active–destructive responding involves actively engaging with the news but in a negative and counterproductive manner. For example, "*You?* Engaged? Is the guy blind or what?" While that's a pretty extreme destructive response, another more subtle but just as damaging response may be, "Oh no, you poor thing. Will you be able to afford a wedding?"

4. **Active–Constructive Responding (Supporting and amplifying excitement):** The most effective response is active–constructive responding, characterized by genuine positive interest and enthusiasm. This involves actively engaging with the person's good news, asking thoughtful questions, and showing a desire and willingness to celebrate together. In our example, such a response may be, "Oh, wow, congratulations! That is such good news. I'm thrilled for you. Oh, I can't wait for you to tell me—what was the proposal like?"

Active–constructive responding involves acknowledging a speaker's emotions and encouraging further sharing through engaged prompts. This approach, described as an "emotional hug" by psychologist Mark Goulston, enhances mutual understanding and positive communication. Destructive and passive reactions, on the other hand, convey disinterest and can lead to poorer communication outcomes and strained relationships. Given what we already know about validation, this makes sense—people communicate not merely because they want to convey some factual information, but because they want to share their *emotional* reality with someone else and have that acknowledged and accepted. If this emotional reality is not reflected, people can feel invisible, unimportant, and unloved, and they even start to second-guess themselves.

Paying attention to your response is important and plays a big role in how much empathy you can feel and convey. Stepping back and allowing people the space to enjoy their good feelings, and supporting them while they do so, sends a powerful message of compassion and respect. Too often, we're happy to play the caring-counselor role when people are unhappy, but unconsciously fail to show up for our loved ones when they're doing well and feeling good. It takes enormous emotional maturity to not be threatened by someone's good fortune or happiness when we're not necessarily feeling that way ourselves. It's a form of "positive empathy" that very seldom gets mentioned!

Here's how you can develop some of it yourself.

## Pay Attention

No surprises here; it's the first step for every communication skill. Wait until someone is sharing good news or excitedly relaying a happy story. Focus entirely on them and their message without diverting the attention to yourself or considering what you personally think and feel about it. Resist the urge to interject with your own experiences or opinions, or give advice.

## Reflect Their Nonverbal Communication

Remember that this form of empathy is about mirroring their emotional experience, and this will come through loud and clear in their posture, voice, physical gestures, and facial expressions. If they're smiling and talking quickly and with plenty of animation, then respond with the same energy and smile back. If they're using a particular tone of voice, phrase, or gesture, show them you've heard the emotional content it signifies by mimicking it yourself.

## Avoid Self-Centered Responses

Refrain from immediately shifting the focus to yourself, your achievements, or your challenges. Steer clear of comparing their news to your own situation or injecting personal anecdotes that may detract from their moment. Basically, the idea is not to center yourself and your opinions. There is a difference, for example, between congratulating someone on their promotion because you're worried about their financial life and congratulating them because you know *they've* been stressed out about money. Keep the spotlight on them and their news.

*Don't* use these words: however, whereas, yet, then again, on the other hand ... and especially BUT. These words and phrases are essentially code for "please ignore everything I said before these words." Imagine how it feels, for example, to be told, "It's so great you've got this promotion. On the other hand, you'll have to work a lot harder now!"

## Delay Questions until They've Finished Their Story

Questions are a great way to show that you're paying attention and you care about the details—but be aware of the kind of questions you're asking and *when*. Allow the person to share their news completely without interruption. Practice patience and let them express themselves fully before asking questions. Otherwise you risk placing a speedbump in the way of their excitement, or subtly implying that they need to explain or justify their news to you somehow.

Encouraging expressions and comments ("Really? Uh huh. Wow!") are usually more appreciated, but if you do ask questions, keep them judgment-free and exploratory—for example, "Tell me more" or "What happens now?"

## Nobody Needs You to Be a Realist or a "Devil's Advocate"

"I won a round-the-world cruise!"

"That's great. It's hell on the environment, but let's not focus on that right now, huh? Is your passport up to date?"

Do you remember the "critical" listening style from a previous chapter? Some people have taken it upon themselves in life to relentlessly deflate other people's excitement and enthusiasm in the name of being practical, realistic, and rational. They mistakenly adopt the position of evaluating and assessing information instead of reacting to the emotional content—and this sometimes comes across as judgmental and pessimistic. This pessimism is often offered to others as a valiant service to them and a helpful corrective to what you clearly think is their own foolishness.

Deep down, this kind of cynical response is actually a passive-aggressive way of trying to dominate and control the conversation, and it's an extremely toxic habit that can alienate people very quickly. The trouble is that you can always claim, "I'm just being reasonable! I'm just trying to help!" but the damage will already be done, and people will intuit your true intentions even if technically you haven't said anything untrue and they can't put a finger on the problem. Try to avoid making unhelpful corrections to irrelevant details or giving warnings and cautions that act like a bucket of cold water poured over people's excitement. Instead, wish people well and celebrate with them—it's more fun!

Of course, we can't always get this process right, and sometimes we just won't be on the same wavelength emotionally as the other person. If you're genuinely distracted or unable to fully listen and reflect, then there's nothing wrong with saying something like, "Hey, I'm so glad for you and I'm really interested to hear more about this, but is it all right if I chat with you later, when I'm not so caught up in work?"

## The Art of Paraphrasing

*In this chapter: Paraphrasing is about so much more than just repeating what you've heard; it's about making an effort to hear the other person's message as fully and clearly as you can.*

Sometimes conflict arises not because people genuinely have different wants and needs, but because one or both partners hasn't properly understood the other. You've probably been in an argument like this yourself: After a while, it becomes clear that the person is arguing with an idea of what they *think* you've said and done, and not really with you!

When tempers are flaring, people feel threatened or confused, or there is some disappointment or hurt feelings. It's all the more difficult to properly process what other people are saying—not to mention it's difficult to express *yourself* when you're feeling this way. Active listening is crucial for effective communication, especially when conveying complex or emotionally delicate thoughts.

When sharing uncertain or vulnerable information, it can be frustrating if the listener immediately offers unsolicited advice or forms conclusions. It can feel as though the other person has taken your unique and nuanced message and squashed it right down to just its basic elements, then responded to *that* rather than what you originally expressed. What happens next is that an argument evolves between two *caricatures* of the people involved instead of a sincere engagement between the two people themselves.

For example, someone says, "I feel a little awkward when you make comparisons between me and other women. I know you're giving me a compliment, but it still feels like you're focusing only on my physical appearance, and that's actually quite nerve-wracking. It makes me feel a little exposed . . . like I'm being appraised. I guess it makes me imagine the possibility that you could one day make that same comparison, but not in my favor."

A poor communicator may respond by saying, "Okay, fine. You don't want me to say you're beautiful, so I won't. How was I to know you're so sensitive about how you look?"

You can immediately see the problem here: It's not the issue at hand, but rather the lack of real listening and the failure to communicate about the issue. The person responding has not only failed to grasp the meaning of the other person's message, but their response is likely to create conflict where there wasn't originally any. The first person might rightly retaliate. "That's *not* what I said."

A more constructive approach is for the listener to first **reflect** what was communicated, providing a paraphrase—a brief but accurate summary of the speaker's message. This paraphrasing technique ensures that the listener actively checks for understanding and helps maintain the connection between the speaker and the listener.

This does two things: It ensures you have in fact heard the other person, but it also communicates that you are interested in making this clarification, i.e., not just assuming that you already understand. If you merely assume that you've grasped the message in full and barge ahead, you risk muddying the waters and creating more confusion and misunderstanding.

Research indicates that while paraphrasing may increase the likability of the listener, it may not significantly impact how understood or satisfied the speaker feels. This is because paraphrasing can be perceived as agreement, fostering a positive impression without necessarily enhancing comprehension or satisfaction. To maximize effectiveness, paraphrasing should be complemented with techniques that address nonverbal cues from the speaker.

Paraphrasing has three types: content, intent, and tone. But before we delve into that, let's tackle the concept of "owned language" and perception-checking questions:

"Owned language" involves using "I" instead of "you" to take responsibility for interpreting a message, placing the burden of understanding on oneself. This approach, employed in paraphrasing, demonstrates one's personal understanding rather than just parroting what the other person said directly, aiming to avoid defensiveness. Examples of "owned language" include phrases like "If I understand you correctly . . ." or "It's my understanding that . . ." Perception-checking questions, typically used at the end of a paraphrase, seek to confirm understanding and include inquiries such as "Am I right?" or "Did I understand that correctly?"

## Paraphrasing for Content:

When paraphrasing for content, the focus is on restating what was said without delving into interpretation or emotions. For instance:

Person A: I'm working late tonight. I need the lawn mowed, the dishes done, and the living room vacuumed before our guests arrive.

Person B: Okay, so I need to mow, finish the dishes, and vacuum. Have I got that right?

## Paraphrasing for Intent:

Paraphrasing for intent involves understanding the *purpose* behind a statement, going beyond the literal content. Consider the example:

Person A: I'm working late tonight. We've got guests coming tonight and the lawn isn't mowed, the dishes haven't been done, and the living room hasn't been vacuumed.

Person B: If I'm understanding you correctly, you're wanting me to do these things so we can entertain the guests tonight. Is that right?

## Paraphrasing for Tone:

Paraphrasing for tone focuses on grasping the *emotional* aspect of a message, considering both verbal and nonverbal cues. In the example:

Person A: I'm working late tonight again. I don't know how the hell you're supposed to keep a tidy house *and* work full time. It's impossible. The guests will arrive soon and think we're pigs, but what can be done?

Person B: It sounds to me like you're pretty overwhelmed and frustrated about this. Is that how you're feeling?

Sometimes, then, we can reflect and paraphrase the nonverbal content of a message, which may not resemble the verbal message at all. We are essentially asking, "Is *this* the message you want to send me right now?" You can probably tell that there is significant overlap between these different ways of "paraphrasing" and indeed a skillful response is often a blend of all three.

## How To Structure a Complete Paraphrase:

1. **Start with owned language.** Avoid defensiveness and focus on demonstrating your personal understanding rather than just stating what the other person said directly. Use phrases like "It sounds to me . . ." "If I understand you correctly . . ." "It's my understanding that . . ." This signals that you're willing to be corrected (hint: if you are corrected, pay attention and adjust accordingly!).
2. **Notice their tone.** Focus on understanding and interpreting the

emotion of the speaker's statement, which will often be expressed nonverbally or merely implied. For example, if they sound or appear anxious or stressed, or they're listing a long string of anxious ideas, mention that they seem stressed.

3. **Look for their intent and restate what they said**. Look beyond what is said and focus on WHY the person said it, and then restate their message using your own words.

4. **Always end with a perception-checking question.** Finish your statements to confirm your understanding. Examples of these inquiries are "Is that right?" "Did I understand it correctly?"

Putting it all together, here's an example:

Person A: I'm working late tonight. I need the lawn mowed, the dishes done, and the living room vacuumed before our guests arrive.

Person B: It sounds to me (owned language) like you are stressed (tone) about this and would like me to help (intent) mow the lawn, finish the dishes, and vacuum before our guests arrive (content). Is that right (perception-checking question)?

Let's take a look at a slightly more complicated example:

Person A: I feel a little awkward when you make comparisons between me and other women. I know you're giving me a compliment, but it still feels like you're focusing only on my physical appearance, and that's actually quite nerve-wracking. It makes me feel a little exposed . . . like I'm being appraised. I guess it makes me imagine the possibility that you could one day make that same comparison, but not in my favor.

Person B: If I've understood this correctly (owned language), you feel uncomfortable (tone) when I give you a compliment that compares you to other women, and you want me to stop (intent). Have I got that right (perception-checking question)?

For an even better and less formulaic response, Person B could register the deeper emotional content of what Person A is expressing, i.e., why they're speaking at all. Does Person A need validation that they are valued and loved for who they are? Do they need assurance about the relationship?

During conflict, good paraphrasing is even more important. Practicing repeating what you've heard in your own words forces you to remove your own interpretations, assumptions, and judgments and remind yourself that the only way to really understand what someone means is to listen to them. If on the other hand you yourself feel that you are not being heard and that the other person is continually misunderstanding you, then feel free to politely say, "I'm sorry but no, I don't think you've understood me." Repeat yourself in a different way and try again. If you are unfortunate to find yourself in a conflict where someone insists on willfully misunderstanding you, then gracefully step away and refuse to engage—no straw man ever won an argument!

## Listening to Solve Problems

*In this chapter: Failing to listen creates problems, but listening can solve them. With real listening, you can quickly find your way back to harmonious connection with the other person.*

With curiosity, we can learn to listen to what *really is*—rather than what we assume is. But we can also use curiosity to listen in a prospective way, i.e., to listen for what *might be*.

Listening well can help us resolve problems and smooth over conflicts because it helps us stay alert to potential solutions and ways forward. When we listen with ego, we may only be able to focus on those things we already believe are true, or we listen defensively, our ears pricked for the slightest hint that we are being attacked or need to prove ourselves. It keeps us trapped exactly where we are.

Have you ever noticed that sometimes people who are having arguments can start to seem pretty childish? It's as though conflict kicks us down a few notches on the maturity scale, and we start a petty back-and-forth that starts to resemble a playground spat rather than a genuine conversation. It's for this reason that we're going to take an approach that was originally designed for adults communicating with children—when we are hurt, defensive, angry, or avoidant, we become the conversational equivalent of toddlers.

So, how do we communicate with children? And how do we make sure that our own communication during conflicts is as mature as possible?

According to the parenting book *How to Talk So Kids Will Listen & Listen So Kids Will Talk*, active listening is a vital part of communication with children. Authors Adele Faber and Elaine Mazlich explain that though their advice is intended for parents trying to interact with their children, the principles they describe actually apply to all interactions between people. Their model is a version of "nonviolent communication" (NVC) that centers harmony, cooperation, and problem-solving.

Communication that works is communication that:

- Foregoes blame, punishment, and recrimination and instead prioritizes mutual well-being
- Tries to find a win-win rather than win-lose outcome (or a zero-sum outcome where someone getting their needs met

implies that someone else must go
without)

- Focus on compassion and connection rather than technique and skill
- Breaks old loops and negative feedback patterns and tries something new

Too often, our approach to communication, especially communication that is failing, is to try to find some little trick or technique that will allow us to control or even manipulate the other person, to fix things (i.e., fix *them*), and to come out on top. Communication can be "violent" without shouting and name-calling. Any time we deny the other person respect or agency or refuse to imagine that their perspective is valid, we are doing them a kind of violence.

Crucially, the authors emphasize that good communication is seldom natural or easy—it takes work and a great deal of practice, so forgiveness and tolerance are necessary as you both work things out together. There are no easy-to-memorize scripts that we can whip out to spare ourselves the messiness of communicating with other people. But just as we learn to be patient and compassionate with those we're trying to connect with, we can also be patient and tolerant with ourselves for not always getting it right!

It's easy to fall into habits of denying people's feelings, giving them advice or lecturing them, trying to find out who is right and going into "investigator" mode, being defensive or going on the attack, confusing compassion for pity, or being overly abstract by philosophizing or psychoanalyzing rather than dealing with the real person sitting in front of you here and now.

No matter the nature of your disagreement or conflict, try to remind yourself of **your ultimate goal: to find some path back to cooperation, empathy, and understanding**. This is easy to do when you're not in conflict, but takes considerable presence of mind to remember when you're feeling threatened, annoyed, or confused. If you're feeling wronged or misunderstood, it's even *more* important to slow down and deliberately make sure your hurt feelings and ego are not guiding your next steps.

We've already covered many useful techniques for creating genuine connection:

- Pay full attention
- Make neutral observations and tentatively label, without judgment, what you've observed

- Share your sincere feelings and needs without blame or shame
- Stay calm, curious, and receptive

Your mindset and attitude during a conflict will make more of a difference than any particular technique or approach you use. Remember that your goal is to find a path of connection back to the person. In conflict, it's easy to forget this and start behaving in ways that suggest a different goal, one that focuses on your needs to the exclusion of the other person's. We may resort to centering ourselves and positioning the other person as inferior in some way—i.e., someone we have to control, correct, or command; someone we have to lecture or moralize to (while we play martyr); someone we see as a villain and therefore deserving of punishment, like name-calling; someone to educate; or someone to study and understand like some bizarre alien species.

These behaviors may temporarily make you feel superior and in control, but they ultimately damage the relationship. The other person is not a problem to solve, but a human being with a perspective and set of needs as valid as yours. It's also not solely up to you to work through the issue—you're both present and capable of working on it together. If you can separate the problem from the people currently embroiled in it, you can begin to see that it's the *both of you versus the problem*, rather than *you versus them*.

This cooperative and solution-focused mindset is a game-changer. It can help steer parents away from a traditional punishment approach that often only results in negativity and mistrust from their children, but it also encourages adults to treat one another better, too.

In adult interactions, active listening emerges as a crucial tool. Like its impact on parent–child relationships, active listening in adult interactions fosters understanding and connection. Bear in mind that most of us have learned our conflict–resolution strategies and the correct way to communicate from childhood. Learning to communicate in a cooperative, nonviolent way not only helps us overcome this original programming, but ensures we don't repeat the same mistakes going forward. We can learn to treat other people as equal, valued partners in resolving issues. When we create room for open dialogue, everyone feels heard and respected no matter what problems are being faced.

### *Undoing Misunderstanding and Conflict One Step at a Time*

Well, so much for theory, but what do you actually **do** when faced with a conflict? You've probably experienced firsthand just how quickly all your high-minded ideals fly out the window when faced with someone who is being difficult, aggressive, or unfair. Here are a few concrete ways to claw your way out of the ego-based threat mindset and into a cooperative, nonviolent one:

## Step 1: Enter into their perspective

If you've been insulted, disrespected, or hurt, your knee-jerk tendency will be to zoom in on these feelings and go on the defensive. Try with all your might to resist this inclination and instead turn your attention outward. You will have a chance to express these feelings and make reasonable requests, but none of that can happen until you both feel as if you've been heard and acknowledged. This is always, always the first step—to let people speak and be heard. Then, problem solving can start. If you jump straight to airing your grievances, you only guarantee that you stay mired in the conflict.

Ask yourself:

*What are they experiencing and feeling right now?*

*What are they trying to achieve with this conversation?*

*What are their unmet needs?*

Invite the other person to share their perspective fully, and listen without judgment, interpretation, or interruption. Let them get their emotional cards on the table. This lets you know what you're dealing with, but also demonstrates your willingness to cooperate and removes much of the sting of the conflict.

Imagine you run a business creating bespoke wedding dresses. Despite carefully explaining your return policies, you have an unhappy client who is demanding a refund. The client has gained weight, and the dress no longer fits; the wedding is in a week and they want another dress made, but such a dress usually takes you a month to create. You're furious and stressed out and resent being put in this position.

Despite your own feelings, though, you try to understand things from your client's perspective. They're probably panicking even more than you are, and they may be embarrassed about the mistake. They also have no idea how a dress is made and how long it takes, so they may be viewing *you* as the obstacle and imagining that you could make a dress faster if only you tried!

## Step 2: Make the speaker feel like a collaborator, not a problem

One of the best ways to get the ball rolling is to actively express your desire to cooperate, not fight. Let them know that you acknowledge and respect their autonomy, and that though you are in a disagreement, you're not in conflict with *them* as people. You want to emphasize that the goal is not about winning or losing but about finding a solution that meets the needs of both sides.

In our example, you remind yourself that although this client is being unfair and difficult, *they* are not the problem—the problem is the problem. All through your conversation you say things like:

"I value all my clients, so I'm eager for **us** to find a way around this."

"Let's figure this out **together**."

"I hope we can find a compromise that works for **both** of us."

## Step 3: Own your side of things

If you've respectfully made efforts to listen to their experiences and needs, you may find that they are far more willing to hear yours. As before, stay neutral and stick to the facts, and when expressing your emotions, make sure to keep them *your* emotions—use "I" statements rather than implying that they are the cause of your feelings.

"I always get special pride out of giving my customers exactly what they want, so I feel disappointed that you're not satisfied. The dress you were given fit the measurements you gave at the time, but the measurements have changed now, and there's not enough time to create a new dress before the wedding." (Note, there is no blame here—you don't mention at all whose "fault" the problem is—it doesn't matter now, right?)

Bear in mind their perspective when making requests or asking for your needs to be met. Your request may feel valid to you, but is it reasonable, given their abilities and resources? Is there some other way for you to get what you want? Could the environment itself or some other factor be adjusted to make things easier for everyone?

## Step 3: Together, brainstorm a way forward

Once you're actively talking about possibilities, you can gently explore possible compromises. If both sides feel that they have been fully heard and respected, they'll be more willing to explore different ways around the issue—ways they wouldn't have considered while still feeling hurt, threatened, or misunderstood. Depending on the size of the issue, you might like to literally sit together and brainstorm a solution. Be open-minded and nonjudgmental, exploring all possibilities, even if some are unrealistic. Collaboratively evaluate and eliminate unworkable ideas to arrive at a compromise solution.

"Now, there's simply no way to make the exact same dress again, I'm afraid. But I think there are lots of other options if we put our heads together. One possibility is that I quickly make a kind of shawl to go over the current dress to conceal the ill-fitting parts. Another option is to buy a new dress in the right size—I have a colleague who lives near you who runs a store and can book you an appointment this afternoon. Or perhaps you have a suggestion . . .?"

**Step 4: Be willing to adjust**

Remember that it will take time. Your first solution may not work, and you may need to come back to the drawing board. Try not to see this as a problem or a trigger to go back into conflict. Expect that the process is ongoing and that adjustments are not a sign that someone is doing something wrong.

In our example, perhaps the customer agrees to the shawl idea but refuses to pay extra for it and won't budge. You cut your losses and agree, but push her for a good review on your site. It's not perfect, but a workable way forward has been found, and most importantly, the relationships are broadly still intact—the customer returns a year later for another dress.

## Summary

- Emotional regulation allows you to own your experience and avoid needless conflict with others. In emotionally overwrought situations, notice any strong feelings emerging and try to gain psychological distance from them. Pause, become aware of what's happening, and gradually challenge your knee-jerk assumptions and biases about the situation.
- Listening is not just about being there to support people who are angry or sad; it's also about knowing how to handle people's joy and excitement. There are four response types: *active and constructive*

(the ideal), *passive and constructive*, *passive and destructive*, and *active and destructive* (the worst). Try to reflect and support people's emotional experience and respond accordingly. Avoiding self-centered or inappropriate responses can reduce conflict.

- Avoid misunderstanding and conflict by paraphrasing to confirm you've genuinely understood someone's full message, especially if tempers are flaring and the topic is complex.
- You can paraphrase content, intent, and emotional tone, but always begin with "owning" language and end with a perception-checking statement to confirm your understanding.
- Listening well can help us resolve problems and smooth over conflicts because it helps us stay alert to potential solutions and ways forward. Prioritize finding a path back to cooperation, empathy, and understanding. Consider their perspective, own our side of things, and brainstorm a solution together, without making them feel like the problem. Be patient, though, because conflict resolution can take time.

# Conclusion

Learning to be a masterful listener is not something that can be achieved overnight. Luckily for us, however, we are all blessed with an entire lifetime in which to practice, and plenty of people of all kinds to practice with!

Skillful listening is really the heart of all communication, and that in turn is an essential part of any relationship, whether that's at work, at home, or with a romantic partner. One of the most curious side effects of improving your listening skills is that you may discover how much more willing other people are to listen to *you*. While this book was not about how to speak so people will listen, the irony is that learning to listen will make you a more likeable person—and in a roundabout way, the kind of person people want to listen to.

Tricks and techniques are not what matters; rather, an entire mindset shift is required. A good listener has learned to approach people, and life itself, in a different way. As you learn to pay attention and to encounter reality as it really is, you may find that your listening skills transfer to all sorts of other areas in your life. You may discover that you are more patient, more creative, more relaxed, and more resilient. All the skills that make us empathetic and perceptive listeners are the same skills we can bring to our work, our dreams, our challenges, and our own self-concept. Listening seems at first like a small, unimpressive thing, but it is not an exaggeration to say that genuine deep listening could change the world.

# Summary Guide

- The first task of listening is to be prepared, receptive, and willing. Good listening requires that we are prepared in the same way as if we were planning to give a speech or write an email. Listening readiness comes in three categories: physical, mental, and emotional. Take care to properly set the stage in each category.
- Listening is not passive and is as important as speaking, requiring as much skill, deliberation, and practice. Most of us receive no training on how to listen, or wrongly assume we don't need to learn. Listening is a skill that can be learned, and the reward is more satisfying communication, better relationships, and less conflict.
- There are four main ways to listen: *appreciative* (focusing on deriving enjoyment from what is being communicated), *empathetic* (showing concern and understanding for the speaker's emotional perspective), *comprehensive* (understanding and processing the informational content of the message), and *critical* (evaluating the

197

content of the message, appraising, and making judgments). All approaches have value; the skill comes with being able to tailor your approach to the unique situation you're in and the other person's needs.

- Pseudo-listening is the mere *appearance* of listening without the deeper attention and receptivity that comes with genuine listening—avoid it!
- Always remember that you have the option to stay silent (that includes mentally). Silence creates space, allows possibilities to unfold, and lets a conversation "breathe."

## CHAPTER 2: ROADBLOCKS TO MASTERFUL LISTENING

- Noise can derail even the best-laid conversational plans. There are four types of noise: *physical* (environmental distractions), *physiological* (biological discomfort and impediments), *semantic* (difficulties understanding the meaning of words or symbols in communication), and *psychological* (emotional overwhelm). Carefully identify potential noise sources and proactively prepare to remove them before listening.

- The closeness-communication bias means that the closer we feel to someone, the less likely we are to listen carefully to them, because our familiarity makes us feel like we already know what they're going to say. Be aware of this and commit to truly listening with an open mind. People change, and you cannot take agreement and similarity as a given.
- Adopt a beginner's mind and drop your assumptions, biases, and expectations. Be clear and open-minded and don't expect others to be mind readers.
- Mentally preparing your response to what someone is telling you while they're telling you increases cognitive strain and decreases the overall attention and brainpower you have to spend on articulating your thoughts and to listening to what you're being told.
- Instead, slow down, listen first, *then* gracefully go into response mode. Be mindful of the media you consume (books, social media, TV, etc.) and how this may be influencing (or undermining) your communication style.

## CHAPTER 3: ASK YOUR EGO TO TAKE A BACK SEAT

- One of the biggest impediments to good listening and communication is the ego. Good communicators are secure, relaxed, humble, respectful, and curious, and see conversations as opportunities to learn, connect, and bond. They don't see difference of opinion as a threat and have no need to compete or convince.
- While the ego has its uses, don't let it get in the way of connection, communication, and collaboration with others. Put yourself in others' shoes, suspend judgment, and recognize that other people occupy different frames of reference.
- Interrupting people while they speak is actually a power play, usually driven by the ego. If you're an interrupter, be mindful of your habit and understand where it comes from, then commit to focusing more on people's words and showing support nonverbally and without interrupting.
- Conversational narcissism is the tendency to center the self in conversation. We are guilty any time we engage in a style of communication that consistently centers our own desires, needs, perspectives, and interests *over* everyone else's. Instead, give praise and take pleasure in other people's achievements, be comfortable with making a fool of yourself sometimes, ask for help

and advice, and forego having or sharing an opinion.

- Everyone craves knowing that they matter, they make sense, they're valued and respected, and they belong. When listening, offer people this validation and verbally normalize their experience.

## CHAPTER 4: CURIOSITY IS KING

- A curious active-listening mindset (CALM) is about genuine curiosity and a deep desire to understand the speaker on a profound level. It requires the suspension of our own perspective, preconceptions, expectations, and judgments so we can encounter theirs. CALM is especially useful for conflict resolution, addressing grievances and issues, negotiation, and giving and receiving feedback in the workplace.
- Be prepared, stick to the facts, paraphrase what you hear, and check to see that you've properly understood. Listen to understand, not to respond. Express yourself respectfully and prioritize collaboration and connection. Calm curiosity diffuses defensiveness and misunderstandings.

- Questions are great, but ask the right ones. Choose thoughtful, polite, exploratory open-ended questions that aren't loaded or delivered as an interrogation. Let them build meaningfully to show genuine interest. Avoid questions about money, people's romantic lives, appearance, and so on.
- Nonverbal communication (voice, body language, appearance, etc.) is just as, if not more so, important as verbal communication. Pay attention to a person's total expression, and reflect this back in your own communication.
- Listen well and you can spot lies more easily; pay attention to the way people use language, and forget about using visual or behavioral cues. Listen closely for inconsistency, hedging, fuzziness, odd use of pronouns, overcompensation, distanced language, and evidence of an increased cognitive load.

## CHAPTER 5: COMMUNICATION AND CONFLICT

- Emotional regulation allows you to own your experience and avoid needless conflict with others. In emotionally overwrought situations, notice any strong feelings emerging and try to gain psychological distance from them. Pause, become aware of what's happening, and gradually challenge your knee-jerk assumptions and biases about the situation.

- Listening is not just about being there to support people who are angry or sad; it's also about knowing how to handle people's joy and excitement. There are four response types: *active and constructive* (the ideal), *passive and constructive*, *passive and destructive*, and *active and destructive* (the worst). Try to reflect and support people's emotional experience and respond accordingly. Avoiding self-centered or inappropriate responses can reduce conflict.

- Avoid misunderstanding and conflict by paraphrasing to confirm you've genuinely understood someone's full message, especially if tempers are flaring and the topic is complex.

- You can paraphrase content, intent, and emotional tone, but always begin with "owning" language and end with a perception-checking statement to confirm your understanding.

- Listening well can help us resolve problems and smooth over conflicts because it helps us stay alert to potential solutions and ways forward. Prioritize finding a path back to cooperation, empathy, and understanding. Consider their perspective, own our side of things, and brainstorm a solution together, without making them feel like the problem. Be patient, though, because conflict resolution can take time.

Printed in the USA
CPSIA information can be obtained
at www.ICGtesting.com
CBHW051736210624
10449CB00011B/746

9 781647 435561

.